THEY COULD NOT TRUST THE KING

NIXON,
WATERGATE,
AND THE
AMERICAN
PEOPLE

Photographs by
STANLEY TRETICK

Text by
WILLIAM V. SHANNON

Foreword by
BARBARA W. TUCHMAN

Collier Books

A Division of
Macmillan Publishing Co., Inc.
NEW YORK

Collier Macmillan Publishers
LONDON

DESIGNED BY
ALLEN HURLBURT

Macmillan Publishing Co., Inc.
866 Third Avenue, New York, N.Y. 10022
Collier-Macmillan Canada Ltd.

They Could Not Trust the King
is published in a hardcover edition by
Macmillan Publishing Co., Inc.

Library of Congress
Catalog Card Number: 72–20374

First Collier Books Edition 1974

Printed in the United States of America

CONTENTS

This book is dedicated
with love
By the photographer
to his wife, Maureen
By the author
to his sons, Liam,
Christopher, and David

AUTHOR'S NOTE:
I am grateful to Stanley Tretick,
who first conceived of this book
and whose photographs inspired
me in the writing of it. I am also
grateful to Maureen Tretick for her
valuable research and to my editor,
Bruce Carrick, and to my wife,
Elizabeth, for their careful and
sensitive reading of the manuscript.

The text for this book was
completed on November 30,
1973, and reflects the evidence
developed up to this date by the
Senate Watergate Committee and
the Special Prosecutor's Office,
as well as President Nixon's
public responses to the evidence.

WILLIAM V. SHANNON
Washington, D.C.
November 30, 1973

PHOTOGRAPHER'S NOTE:
I would like to thank the following
members of the staff of N.B.C.
Nightly News, at whose commission I took the photographs that
made this book possible:
John Chancellor, Lester M. Crystal,
Richard Fischer, Paul Friedman,
and Joseph Angotti.

STANLEY TRETICK
Washington, D.C.
November 30, 1973

Concerning the Long Parliament and King Charles I:

"They could not trust the king. He had no doubt passed salutary laws; but what assurance was there that he would not break them? He had renounced oppressive prerogatives; but where was the security that he would not resume them? The nation had to deal with a man whom no tie could bind . . ."
—*from Macaulay's essay on Milton*

FOREWORD

by Barbara W. Tuchman

The faces portrayed in these pages separate into three groups: the Senators, the witnesses, and the public. Each reveals a different aspect of the tragedy that has been uncovered beneath the glossy surface of American life. Skulduggery and dirty tricks, even tax evasion and misuse of public funds are not the tragedy, except insofar as they illustrate to what level the United States has sunk. The central issue of the crisis is the abuse of Executive power; the danger lies in the habit of acquiescence. These problems are as yet unresolved but the tragedy has already happened. It is history's recurring tragedy of a country's decline from the bright hopes and high intentions of great beginnings.

As chairman, symbol, and conscience of the Select Committee, Senator Ervin exemplified the knowledge of what we have lost. His sense of Constitutional structure and the sincerity of his outrage at its violation was what gave the Committee importance and transformed the hearings into a political lesson. He was as at home in the Constitution as in his own house; the Bill of Rights was as close to him as a wife. The value he set upon them gave the hearings a principle. It is both sad and significant that the oldest member of the Committee was the one who best appreciated the strengths of our system as well as the threat to them.

The witnesses, all of them officials or agents of the Nixon Administration, left a stunning impression of something missing—some ordinary, familiar component of the human makeup, taken for granted when present but sinister by its absence. Leaving aside differences of personality and position, collectively the cohorts of Mr. Nixon were deficient, like the Man Without a Shadow, in an attribute the human being is supposed to have. They were without a sense of wrong.

As they took the stand one after another to describe or defend their conduct, the viewer was awed at the revealed willingness and readiness to undertake wrongdoing. Whether the proposed operation was illegal, immoral, unethical, criminal, or dirty trick, few hesitated, only one ever said No. If doubts ever assailed one of these men or private standards whispered in his ear, they did not at any time prevail.

Inability to distinguish between right and wrong used to be the judicial definition of insanity. It has been abandoned because, I suppose, twentieth-century man is so unsure of the difference between the two that he does not wish to dispose of another man's life or freedom by so blurred a criterion. Humanly if not judicially, however, there is some sense in the idea that a person who does not recognize wrong has something wrong with him. One cannot deal with him because he has no inhibitions, just as one cannot play tennis or any other game with a person who does not know or will not stay within the rules.

The witnesses' casual contempt for society's rules, including the Ninth Commandment—"Thou shalt not bear false witness against thy neighbor"—was so untroubled as almost to suggest ignorance. One wondered, where did they go to school? Who were their parents, their teachers and pastors? Did all of them somehow skip what used to be called Civics in the eighth grade?

In formulating that question one begins to understand the nature of the tragedy. These men are not peculiar to the Nixon White House (although it evidently attracted a high concentration of the raw arrogance of the parvenu). They are what has happened to America and to our time. The same contempt for the rules is visible in street people who relieve themselves on doorsteps, and muggers who murder without a blush, and Mets fans who treat a visiting team throughout with howling hostility and swarm like a lynch mob over the field, trampling on people in their eagerness to wreck and vandalize. Conventions such as fair play and courtesy have evolved in the long civilizing process up from savagery in order to make human society bearable, just as political rules and the laws of life and property have evolved in order to make it safe. Without conventional restraints man becomes dangerous or unpleasant whether in the White House or in Shea Stadium.

Dr. Karl Menninger has diagnosed this phenomenon of our time as the absence of a sense of sin. Perhaps the sins of the twentieth century have been so great that in self-defense we have rejected the concept of sin in favor of the easier principle of anything goes. Yet a sense of sin is necessary for order, and man's whole history has been a search for order. No amount of police, courts, and prisons can make society's controls work if the individual conscience is inoperative.

I come now to the third element—the public. The faces portrayed here are grave; the expression is one of wonderment, worry, a touch of fear. Perhaps the same look was on the faces waiting outside the grand jury room in 1920 when the great batter, Shoeless Joe Jackson, idol of the fans, was indicted with eight members of the Chicago White Sox for conspiring with gamblers to throw the 1919 Series to the Cincinnati Reds. "Say it ain't so, Joe!" pleaded the small boy who has gone down in legend. (According to newspaper accounts, the actual words of a group of boys were, "It's not true, is it, Joe?" to which his reply was, "Yes, boys, I'm afraid it is.")

That anxiety not to damage the image was clearly apparent in public opinion about Watergate in the period prior to the crisis of October 1973. If there was any dominant sentiment, it was reluctance to believe ill of the President and a desperate desire to sweep all the horrid doings under the rug and let him maintain his fiction of untainted rectitude. Americans have an overdeveloped tendency to president-worship. The public *wants* to believe that the president—any president—is good. This comes, I think, from our frustrated craving for a figurehead. Other Western democracies allow themselves either a monarch or a long-term president to absorb worship from the working premier, but we put worship where the power is, which is an unwise arrangement.

Moreover, we lack a historical past with the tall shadows of myths and legends and heroes that European and Asian peoples feel standing behind them. When we banished King George in 1776, we unfortunately also banished King Arthur. This leaves a great floating body of sentiment to settle on the Chief Executive whoever he may be.

11

When that investment of trust is shaken, as by Watergate, a large segment of the population becomes exceedingly nervous, like passengers on a plane if told the pilot is drunk. They must believe in the man at the top, otherwise who is going to take care of them? The fact that the man at the top has been cutting into their Constitutional rights is of secondary concern because most people would rather be taken care of than be free.

How the turning point comes when mistrust of the pilot can no longer be suppressed. History will place that point in the President's extraordinary maneuver in October to stop the wheels of judgment from running over him, following as it did hard upon the disgrace of his twice-chosen running mate while holding national office. Loss of confidence in the authorities means a perilous time for society. When the medieval Church lost popular esteem and sank into contempt for its corruption and greed, the protest that was to break it apart became inevitable. If faith in the political principles that have been our foundation is undermined, we are unlikely to improve on what Jefferson and his colleagues gave us.

How the crisis will evolve cannot be foretold in mid-October when this Foreword is being written. I can only record what has been my own belief since last July: that President Nixon will not—and should not—complete his term. First, because illegality is so normal to his Administration that there will be no bottom to the findings; second, because in falsifying the war in Cambodia and authorizing the Domestic Intelligence Gathering Plan of 1970 he committed impeachable offenses quite apart from Watergate and defiance of the courts; third, because if we do not bring this abuse of power to account, we will have laid a precedent of acquiescence—what the lawyers call constructive condonement—that will end by destroying the political system whose 200th birthday we are about to celebrate. It may be a flawed system full of corruption and oppressions, but those who become impatient with it and yearn for totalitarian certainties of the Right or of the Left, will never know its value until they lose it.

12

What it comes down to is what Macaulay in his essay on Milton called "the naked Constitutional question." The question, he wrote, was this: "Had Charles the First broken the fundamental laws of England? No person can answer in the negative, unless he refuses credit, not merely to all the accusations brought against Charles by his opponents, but to the narratives of the warmest Royalists and to the confessions of the King himself." The other side asks, he continues, why could not the Parliament have adopted some measure milder than regicide?—for which read impeachment. Macaulay's answer was, "They could not trust the King."

THEY COULD NOT TRUST THE KING

the first time in history, an American president has been seriously
accused of participation while in office in major crimes that, if proved
in a court of law, could result in his being sentenced to several terms
in prison. These crimes include conspiracy to commit breaking, entering,
and burglary, obstruction of a criminal investigation, suborning of
perjury, and misprision of felony. Richard Nixon stands accused
of using a team of secret police to violate the rights of private citizens
and then of using the CIA, the FBI, and the powers of the presidency to
obstruct justice.

      Accusation is not proof. But neither do the President's speeches,
statements, and news-conference answers on Watergate add up to
a convincing refutation. After the first denial on August 29, 1972,
each successive Nixon explanation conceded somewhat more ground on
the charges and contradicted a part of what he had said previously.
In columnist Nicholas von Hoffman's phrase, he sounded like a man
"lying his way toward the truth." Moreover, throughout the summer
and fall of 1973, Nixon carefully stayed away from Senate hearings, grand
juries, or courtrooms, where he would have to testify under oath.
He talked of "turning the matter over to the courts," but his long
legal fight against release of the tapes of White House conversations
showed how determined he was to withhold from the courts what
might be the best evidence on many disputed points.

      In the absence of a legal forum where Nixon could be
examined and his testimony weighed against that of other witnesses,
the public depended upon the televised hearings of the Senate
Watergate Committee to lay out as many of the facts as it could discover.
The Senate created the Select Committee on Presidential Campaign
Activities under the chairmanship of Senator Sam J. Ervin, Jr., of
North Carolina on February 7, 1973. The Committee began its public
hearings three months later on May 17. The first phase of its inquiry
concentrated on the two crucial elements in the Watergate story.
First, there were the attitudes, policies, and activities of the Nixon
Administraton that resulted in the arrest of five of its agents inside the

Chairman Ervin's gavel

headquarters of the Democratic National Committee in the Watergate complex on the night of June 16-17, 1972. Secondly, there was the Administration's subsequent effort—through perjured testimony, payments of hush money, and offers of clemency—to cover up the links between those minor agents and the real men of power. It is on these crucial elements that this book also concentrates. By contrast, the campaign "dirty tricks" were a secondary effect and the campaign financial irregularities a secondary cause of the Watergate conspiracy.

The Committee heard thirty-seven witnesses in thirty-five days of public hearings, including all but two of the major figures. One of the missing was Charles Colson, formerly special counsel to the President, who pleaded the Fifth Amendment in closed session and was not called as a public witness. The other was Richard Nixon, who was invited to appear but declined.

The Senate hearings proved that the White House had organized a campaign of espionage and sabotage against its political opposition that has no parallel in American politics. Lists of enemies were compiled and a rudimentary effort begun to use the powers of the federal government to harass, intimidate, and discredit leaders of the opposition party, the press, the business community, and private citizens as diverse as Arthur Schlesinger, Jr., Joe Namath, Leonard Bernstein, and Eugene Carson Blake. Covert techniques of "black intelligence" used by the CIA, FBI, and military intelligence in previous administrations against foreign espionage agents and domestic radicals of the Far Left and Far Right were deployed under Nixon for political purposes against ordinary American citizens. To finance both its open and undercover political efforts, the Administration raised an unprecedentedly huge fund, partly by putting corrupt pressure on business corporations having tax, regulatory, contractual, or other difficulties with the government.

When agents of the President's campaign organization were arrested in the Watergate, therefore, they were not engaged in a "third-rate burglary," as Ron Ziegler, the White House press spokesman, first described it. They were carrying out an assignment in a complex and far-reaching political plan that could serve as dress rehearsal for an American fascist coup d'etat. Senator Lowell Weicker of Connecticut, a member of the President's own party and a member of the Senate Select Committee, said those who masterminded this plan "were trying to steal America."

The unsuccessful burglary at the Watergate was not an isolated event. It was neither the first such operation nor was it scheduled to be the last. Three weeks earlier, the same men had broken into the Democratic National Committee offices to place taps on telephones and search through the files for whatever might be politically embarrassing. They had also "cased" the campaign headquarters of Senator George McGovern, but had temporarily abandoned their planned break-in. Had they gone undetected in their second Watergate mission, they were scheduled to return to the McGovern headquarters to "bug" it as well as the hotel suites of all the presidential candidates at the Democratic National Convention

20

in Miami Beach.

When the Watergate burglars were arrested, the White House moved quickly to contain the damage. The objective was to cover up the fact that this illegal intelligence-gathering operation had probably been cleared by the President's campaign organization and his senior White House aides and may even have had his prior approval. On Mr. Nixon's own initiative, the Central Intelligence Agency was used as a catspaw to try to head off the Federal Bureau of Investigation's inquiry into how the Watergate burglars were financed by Nixon campaign money—money that was tainted from its source. Part of it was a Minnesota businessman's contribution of $25,000 in cash that had not been reported under the new campaign expenditure law. The rest was a portion of $100,000 from a Texas oil company that may have been an illegal use of corporation funds and that had been "laundered" through Mexico City to make it hard to trace. The President used the CIA to tell the FBI not to trace the source of this money on the grounds that it might inadvertently compromise a secret intelligence operation in Mexico. This diversionary maneuver broke down after two weeks when L. Patrick Gray III, the acting FBI Director, became convinced the CIA had no interest in the matter. But during those two weeks following the break-in and arrests, Nixon campaign officials gained the time needed to work out among themselves plausible explanations of how the money had been handled.

The President at that time also arranged for John N. Mitchell's nominal resignation as his campaign manager, "nominal" inasmuch as the Senate Watergate Committee by analyzing Mitchell's appointment calendar proved that he saw as many campaign officials in the three months after he quit as he did in the three prior months. He did not resign to spend more time with Martha. The apparent purpose of the resignation was to enable Mitchell to devote time to organizing the cover-up, while Clark MacGregor, his successor, devoted himself to the routine public relations aspects of the job. Mitchell's appointment calendar for July, August, and September, 1972, showed that he spent

the bulk of his time in meetings with individuals—John Dean, Jeb Stuart Magruder, and Fred LaRue—who later confessed to being participants in the cover-up.

The cover-up involved perjured testimony at the trial of the Watergate burglars by Magruder, the deputy director of the Committee to Reelect the President, and by Herbert Porter, the committee's director of scheduling. It also involved the payment of large sums of money to the Watergate defendants to induce them to keep silent about the involvement of higher-ups. These transfers of money were initially handled by Herbert Kalmbach, the President's personal attorney, and Anthony Ulasewicz, a retired New York City policeman who had been on the President's private payroll since 1969 to "dig for dirt" about Administration opponents. Subsequently, the cover-up included promises to the defendants that if they agreed to keep their mouths shut and serve in prison for a year or so, President Nixon would grant them pardons. One of those who conveyed these offers of clemency was John Caulfield, another former New York City policeman who had also been doing undercover work for the White House since 1969.

A cover-up was thought to be necessary during the President's reelection campaign because it would have been embarrassing to Mr. Nixon if the public learned that his campaign manager approved the burglary and wiretapping, his finance chairman financed them, and his chief of staff, H. R. Haldeman, received copies of the wiretap information distributed under the code name "Gemstone."

But the White House had more to cover up than the involvement of the President's closest political associates in the burglary and wiretapping. A good deal of other "dirty work" had to be concealed.

There were, for example, the activities of E. Howard Hunt, the ex-CIA agent and prolific author of spy novels, who had recruited the Watergate burglars and was himself one of the defendants. Hunt had been on the White House payroll as a "consultant" in 1971-72. One of his undercover tasks was the doctoring of secret State Department cables to create the false impression that President John F. Kennedy ordered the murder of President Diem of South Vietnam in 1963. These fake cables were to be "leaked" to the press in the event that Senator Edward M. Kennedy became the Democratic presidential nominee against Mr. Nixon.

Hunt was also the central figure in a sinister White House plot to "get" Daniel Ellsberg. The objective was to make it appear that in passing the Pentagon Papers to *The New York Times* and other newspapers, Ellsberg was not acting as a former "hawk" who had become conscience-stricken and obsessed about the Vietnam War but, rather, as an agent of the Soviet Union. A copy of the Pentagon Papers was mysteriously handed over to the Soviet Union three days after publication in *The Times* began. The FBI investigated and determined that neither Ellsberg nor any of his friends had any part in passing the papers to the Soviet embassy. Mysteriously, however, the FBI came up with no evidence of who might have done so.

A telephone conversation between Colson and Hunt on July 1, 1971, one day after the Supreme Court ruled in favor of permitting the publication of the Pentagon Papers in the presss, gives the flavor of White House thinking at that time. Colson tape-recorded the conversation and this tape later came into the possession of the Senate Watergate Committee.

In the phone conversation, Colson speculated that the Pentagon Papers affair "could go one of two ways. Ellsberg could be turned into a martyr of the New Left—he probably will be anyway—or it could become another Alger Hiss case, were the guy exposed and other people . . . operating with him, and this may be the way to really carry it out. We might be able to put this bastard into a hell of a situation and discredit the New Left."

Colson asked Hunt whether "you think that with the right resources employed that this thing could be turned into a major public case against Ellsberg and co-conspirators."

Hunt responded that he thought this was possible "with the proper resources."

"I think the resources are there," Colson continued. "Your answer would be we should go down the line to nail the guy cold."

"Go down the line to nail the guy cold, yes," Hunt replied.

Colson, after further conversation, told Hunt that the Ellsberg case "won't be tried in the court" but "in the newspapers," and added: "So it's going to take some resourceful engineering . . ."

Hunt replied, "I want to see the guy hung, if it can be done to the advantage of the Administration."

Colson: "I think it can be done. I think there are ways to do it, and I don't think this guy is operating alone."

Hunt: "Well, of course, he isn't operating alone. He's got a congeries of people who are supporting him, aiding and abetting him, there's no question about it."

Colson: "But I'm not so sure it doesn't go deeper than that."

Hunt: "Oh, really? You're thinking of like [National Democratic Chairman Lawrence] O'Brien or . . ."

Colson: "Oh, no, I'm thinking of the enemy . . ."

Hunt: "The real enemy. Well, of course, they stand to profit . . . the most, no question about it. You've got codes and policymaking apparatus stripped bare for public examination, all that sort of thing."

Colson forwarded the tape of this conversation to Haldeman with the recommendation that Hunt be placed on the White House staff. Haldeman told Colson to put Hunt in touch with John D. Ehrlichman and "if Ehrlichman likes him, go ahead and hire him."

Ehrlichman interviewed Hunt on July 7, 1971, and approved of him immediately. That same day, Ehrlichman telephoned General Robert E. Cushman, then the deputy director of CIA, and requested him to provide Hunt with the "resources" he needed to carry out his unspecified mission for the White House. In his covering memorandum to Haldeman enclosing the telephone conversation transcript, Colson wrote: "Needless to say, I did not even approach what we had been talking about, but merely sounded out his own ideas."

Two years later, when *The Washington Star-News* printed portions of this transcript, Colson said that what he and Haldeman had been talking about was the possibility of hiring Hunt "to come on to the White House staff to coordinate research on the Pentagon Papers and serve as liaison with the Hill."

Notwithstanding this ingenious explanation, Hunt was never seen on Capitol Hill and the "research" he coordinated was of a very special kind. His assignment was to fabricate as damaging a case against Ellsberg as possible. The "right resources" that he needed were the standard equipment for a spy that the CIA made available to him. In his quest for "research" about Ellsberg, Hunt in September 1971 participated in the break-in of the office of Dr. Lewis Fielding, who had been Ellsberg's psychiatrist in Los Angeles.

This break-in was one of several operations in which Hunt participated along with David Young, Egil Krogh, and G. Gordon

Liddy, the members of the White House Special Investigating Unit, known as "the plumbers." When Hunt, Liddy, and others were arrested in the Watergate break-in, Nixon was determined to protect them because he feared that otherwise they might disclose their involvement in the Ellsberg case and other operations. As late as March 1973, while the Ellsberg trial was in session, Assistant Attorney General Henry Petersen informed the President about the burglarizing of Dr. Fielding's office. Nixon quickly replied: "I know about that. That is a national security matter. You stay out of that. Your mandate is to investigate Watergate." It was only under heavy pressure from Petersen and Richard G. Kleindienst, then the Attorney General, that Nixon agreed to let the Justice Department inform the judge in the Ellsberg trial about the burglary. Unknown to Petersen and Kleindienst, Nixon was secretly attempting to entice the judge with an offer of the FBI directorship. When the judge heard of the burglary of Dr. Fielding's office, he dismissed the case against Ellsberg and his codefendant on the grounds that the pattern of governmental misconduct had precluded a fair trial.

The Watergate burglary was like a loose thread. When pulled, it unraveled a whole pattern of illegality within the Nixon Administration.

A president's character is his country's fate. Another kind of man taking over the presidency in 1969 in a time of war, inflation, youthful unrest, and political disillusionment could have turned the nation's energies and talents into different, constructive paths. But Richard Nixon's character, his reactionary philosophy, and his political commitments foredoomed the nation to corruption and hypocrisy, to a politics of lawless and demagogic manipulation, and to ever-deeper disillusionment as disappointment edged close to despair.

The presidency that Nixon inherited was a more powerful office than any man had ever occupied. Like all of his predecessors since 1945, Nixon had it in his power to order the use of bombs that could destroy the civilized world. "This unimaginable inflation in the powers of the presidency," as *The New York Times* editorially described it, "has worked like yeast to transform the character of the modern presidency, giving it a uniqueness, an awesomeness, an almost mysterious character that the pre-1945 presidency never had."

But it was also a presidency that was slipping out of democratic accountability and control. For nearly thirty years, the American people and their government had been engaged in military and political combat on a world scale. They had fought World War II, two sizable land wars in Korea and Vietnam, and an unremitting "cold war" against the Soviet Union and, for much of the time, against mainland China. So long a struggle against so many diverse enemies had profoundly altered the nation's institutions of government. An enormous military establishment had developed, as well as several large intelligence-gathering bureaucracies, other agencies dispensing foreign economic and military aid and overseas information, and a much-enlarged Federal Bureau of Investigation to guard against foreign spies and domestic Communists. As successive presidents led the way in the creation or expansion of these war and cold-war agencies, the people increasingly relied upon one man— the president—to keep these bureaucracies under democratic and civilian control. But who was to control the president?

The pressures of war inherently move presidents to act in secret and tempt them to act by quick but extraconstitutional means. Franklin D. Roosevelt started this dangerous trend in 1940 when he swapped fifty American destroyers to Britain in exchange for air and naval bases in Bermuda and the British West Indies. He made this swap on the shakiest constitutional authority rather than lose time and imperil Britain's survival by submitting it to the Senate as a treaty. But at least Roosevelt acted openly after encouraging public debate on the idea and gaining the prior consent of Wendell Willkie, then the presidential candidate of the opposition party.

Throughout 1941, up to the very eve of Pearl Harbor, Roosevelt, while professing his devotion to peace, took an increasingly aggressive and unneutral posture toward both Germany and Japan. Yet he held back from asking Congress for the declaration of war that he feared he might not get or that might only be forthcoming after an angry, divisive debate.

Walter Lippmann wrote of Roosevelt's cautious maneuvering during that difficult year: "In this tremendous time the American people must look to their President for leadership. They are not getting leadership from the President. They are not being treated as they deserve to be treated and as they have a right to be treated. They are not being treated as men and women but rather as if they were inquisitive children. They are not being dealt with seriously, truthfully, responsibly, and nobly. They are being dealt with cleverly, indirectly, even condescendingly, and nervously."

It was an adverse judgment that many commentators, including Lippmann, would have occasion to render against later presidents, most notably Lyndon Johnson and Richard Nixon.

In the postwar period, as the United States turned from combatting the totalitarianism of Adolf Hitler to combatting that of Joseph Stalin and his successors, presidents Truman and Eisenhower approved of secret operations in foreign countries to counter equally secret moves by the ideological enemy. Sometimes the operation was as simple as bribing a foreign labor union leader whose strikes were holding up Marshall Plan deliveries. Sometimes it was as complex as restoring the Shah of Iran to power in 1951 or overthrowing the government of Guatemala in 1954. Both presidents committed armed forces to perilous ventures overseas without express Congressional consent: Truman came to the Republic of Korea's assistance in 1950 and Eisenhower intervened in the murky politics of Lebanon in 1958.

The tragedy of Vietnam that came to dominate American life in the last half of the 1960's began as yet another counterstroke to Communist power. There was the dispatch of military and economic aid under Eisenhower, then the sending of military advisers and increased political intervention under Kennedy, and finally a large-scale military commitment under Johnson. From the first, Johnson concealed the scale and direction of his commitment in order to protect his domestic social program from the Congressional attack that befalls any controversial reform program in time of war. As Vietnam grew in unpopularity, Johnson resorted increasingly to dissimulation and defiance. The "credibility gap" opened up and popular disillusionment came rushing in. Vietnam crippled Johnson's administration. Yet until he voluntarily relinquished his chance to seek reelection, Vietnam showed that an American president could begin a sizable war without the prior consent of Congress and steadily escalate that war despite the opposition of half of the Senate and a considerable section of the people.

It was this presidency that Richard Nixon inherited in 1969, a presidency awesome in its potential for nuclear destruction, almost unmanageable in the scope and complextity of its worldwide military, diplomatic, and economic responsibilities, and charged with the supervision of huge but little-known national security bureaucracies operating at home and overseas. Despite growing public uneasiness, the presidency was still a repository of the people's trust and a focus of their hope for morally sound national leadership. Yet it was, as *The Times* observed, an office "become bloated, unresponsive, unduly secretive, out of touch with the people and perhaps even with reality." It was clearly time for a redefinition of relationships, for a new accommodation between the swollen power of the presidency and the shrunken authority of Congress, between the nation's badly strained constitutional practices and the people's need to know about and to control their country's destiny.

In personal terms, Nixon is a Horatio Alger success story. He rose in seven years from an unknown Navy lieutenant in 1946 to Vice President of the United States in 1953. Since then, for more than twenty years, he has been wholly concerned with acquiring and holding the office of president. His career has been a triumph of shrewd intelligence and stubborn will. But it has been a cold and lonely quest. The most sympathetic biographers have searched in vain for the appealing quirk, the touching anecdote, the human foible, the commitment to an idea or a cause larger than himself. They have found only a ravaging ambition, a chilling calculation of today's opportunities and possibilities, a thin, synthetic amiability. There is no relaxed private self and no morally disinterested higher self.

Nixon is one of many anarchic individualists worshiping the success cult in American life. Although not unknown in politics, such individualists are more common in business, where the material rewards are greater and the ladders to success more certain. Had he not run for Congress almost by chance in 1946, Nixon might well have found wealth and professional success as a corporation lawyer or in business. The cult of success is a debased version of the Protestant ethic. It holds that salvation is wholly an individual matter, that material success is the fruit of virtue, and therefore that it is a proof of godliness. The serious flaw in this ethic is its defective sense of the community. A gospel so strongly oriented to individual effort and attainment is weak when it comes to setting moral limits in politics, a sphere where individual success—the victory of one candidate—is far less important than the welfare of all. As Arthur Schlesinger, Jr., has observed, "Politics is not a means of rewarding personal virtue. It is above all a means of meeting public necessities and fulfilling public hopes."

It seems paradoxical that Nixon, who leads a blameless personal life, who does not smoke or play cards or womanize, who drinks sparingly and is a devoted family man, is known to his opponents in politics as "Tricky Dick." Yet the disjuncture between private virtue and public amorality is inherent in this individualist ethic. Evil is thought of as due to an individual's personal shortcomings; it has no social dimension. It is not due, for example, to immoral social arrangements such as monopolistic economic power, the maldistribution of wealth, inferior education, or unjust racial practices. By the same line of logic, a politician who does not smoke, drink, or get convicted of bribe-taking is thought of as ethical even though he may use his political power to perpetuate slums or to keep Mexican-American youngsters at stoop labor in the San Joaquin fields for fourteen hours a day when they should be in school. Politics, in short, becomes a theater for the acting-out of purely personal ambitions. Social philosophy and ethical constraints are secondary, if they matter at all.

Totally dedicated to success in his chosen field of politics, Nixon rarely permits personal distractions to interfere with the concentration and deep personal discipline that success requires. Neither does he scruple to accept political support from a corrupt labor leader like Jimmy Hoffa or a racist like Strom Thurmond or to accept political money wherever it comes from.

Nixon's political base reinforces this individualist ethic. He has been the spokesman for the nouveau riche war contractors, land developers, and speculators of Southern California and, in later years, of the whole "sunshine belt" stretching from Florida to Texas and Arizona. In his four years in the House and two years in the Senate, Nixon compiled a dreary record of subservience to every reactionary interest. He voted against public housing and rent control, against public power and rural electrification projects, against an excess profits tax in the Korean War, against rules changes in the House to make passage of civil rights legislation easier, and against extension of Social Security. Walter Lippmann observed early on, "By his general political formation and his impulses, Mr. Nixon is not an Eisenhower Republican. When he is on his own, he moves toward the Republican right wing."

Only after he was safely reelected in 1972 did Nixon disclose how thoroughly reactionary he is in social outlook. Only then did he set out to dismantle the antipoverty program, impound funds for medical research and water-pollution control, and destroy housing, education, and health programs in the name of a "new federalism." But since a frankly reactionary philosophy evokes many political difficulties in a state like California and in the nation, Nixon had much earlier learned how to camouflage his opinions, to distract attention, to exploit fears and anxieties. In short, he had become a practiced demagogue. The deception and cynicism inherent in demagoguery were the basic cause of Watergate.

During the first two-thirds of his public career, Nixon focused on the single issue of communism. It used to be a wonderful subject for demagoguery because, like heart disease or the gypsy moth, nobody is for it and many fear it. It served perfectly the negative style of politics Nixon has always preferred. He had early acquired an astute teacher in the black art of negative politics in the person of Murray Chotiner, a Los Angeles attorney and political operator. Chotiner outlined his basic techniques at a political workshop for Republican state chairmen in the fall of 1955. *The New York Times* on May 13, 1956, published a portion of the transcript of this off-the-record talk:

"Like it or not, the American people in many instances vote against a candidate, against a party, or against an issue, rather than for . . ." Chotiner observed.

Nixon put that precept into effect in his first campaign for the House against Democratic incumbent Jerry Voorhis. Nixon built his campaign around the theme of Voorhis's "pro-Communism." *Life* magazine later analyzed that first Nixon campaign:

Voorhis was a strong New Dealer, but nothing that he had ever said or done could be remotely mistaken for pro-Communism. Nevertheless Nixon managed to equate him with Communism by using the slogan, "A vote for Nixon is a vote against the PAC [and] its Communist principles."

Now the facts of the matter are these. The regional PAC [the Political Action Committee of the CIO] had fallen under the influence of Communists, but it had not endorsed Voorhis for the clear and simple reason that he had been outspokenly anti-Communist. As the West Coast Communist paper, *People's World,* had complained editorially, "Voorhis is against unity with Communists on any issue under any circumstances." . . . Yet, in such a far-fetched and roundabout way as this, Nixon established in the minds of many voters the belief, or at least the suspicion, that Voorhis had allied himself with the Communists.

Another of Chotiner's stated theories: "Sometimes color has a lot to do with the campaign." Recalling Nixon's campaign for the Senate against Helen Gahagan Douglas in 1950, Chotiner said, "In consulting with the printer, we wanted a different color . . . and in the stock we found a piece of paper that had a pinkish tinge to it and for some reason or other it just seemed to appeal to us for the moment." That was the origin of the famous "pink sheet" that was distributed throughout California and that linked Mrs. Douglas's voting record with that of Representative Vito Marcantonio of New York, a member of the pro-Communist American Labor Party. The pink sheet stated that "Mrs. Douglas and Marcantonio have been members of Congress together since January 1, 1945. During that period Mrs. Douglas voted the same as Marcantonio 354 times. . . ."

Of these votes, the nonpartisan Editorial Research Reports concluded that only 66 were on substantive issues. Of those, Mrs. Douglas and Marcantonio voted 53 times on the same side as either the majority of the House or the majority of the Democratic members. In other words, Mrs. Douglas as a liberal Democrat was in the mainstream of her party voting for measures recommended by presidents Roosevelt and Truman and the Democratic leadership in the House. Yet Nixon repeatedly referred to her throughout the campaign in these terms: "My opponent is a member of a small clique which joins the notorious party-liner Vito Marcantonio in voting time after time against measures that are for the security of this country."

A third Chotiner technique is to introduce one's pet topic by pretending that one has been warned not to discuss it: "You will be amazed at the popular response to such a method. In case after case [in his 1950 campaign] Dick Nixon told audiences 'I have been advised not to talk about communism; but I am going to tell the people of California the truth. . . .' "

When he moved to the national scene as Vice President in the

Eisenhower Administration, Nixon transposed these Chotiner techniques to his new setting. There were the negative personal attacks that were to make his name notorious: "Harry Truman is a traitor to the high principles of the Democratic Party." And: "[Adlai] Stevenson himself has no backbone training. Stevenson holds a Ph.D. degree from Acheson's college of cowardly communist containment—the State Department."

In 1954, he advised Republican candidates for the House to answer every criticism with an attack. "If he asks you where you stand on Dulles, ask him where he stands on Acheson."

That same year, Nixon again pretended to show courage by talking about communism. Thus, in Cheyenne, Wyoming, he said, "It is time to talk frankly and bluntly about the most sinister element of this campaign to date. Why is the Communist Party of the United States fighting so desperately and openly for the defeat of the Republican candidates . . . for the election of an anti-Eisenhower Congress?"

His listeners may have had some difficulty imagining that Communists were "fighting desperately" in the mountains of Wyoming against the GOP and on behalf of such a patently moderate Catholic politician as Senator Joseph C. O'Mahoney.

Throughout the 1954 campaign, Nixon, as the Eisenhower Administration's chief partisan spokesman, set the political theme. He stressed the government's employee security program in which persons of dubious reliablity had allegedly been weeded out. On October 1, 1954, in Bergen County, New Jersey, Nixon said: "We've been kicking out the Communists, the fellow travelers, and the security risks by the thousands."

When the accuracy of that statement was challenged, Nixon reiterated it. On October 6 in Denver, Colorado, he said: "My statement is correct. I didn't shoot from the hip."

In Phoenix, Arizona, on October 24, he said: "The Truman Administration cleared and hired these people. The Eisenhower Administration investigated and fired them." The next day in Las Vegas,

Nevada, he said that if the Democrats won, "the security risks which have been fired by the Eisenhower Administration will all be hired back."

As the campaign ended, Nixon in Denver on November 2 stepped up the intensity and precision of his attack: "Ninety-six percent of the 6,926 Communists, fellow travelers, sex perverts, people with criminal records, dope addicts, drunks, and other security risks removed under the Eisenhower security program were hired by the Truman Administration. What are they trying to cover?"

After the 1954 election, inquiries by newspapermen and public hearings by two Senate committees unearthed facts about the security program quite at variance with Nixon's statements. Ninety percent of the "security risks" had been fired under routine civil service procedures and not under the new security program, although their dismissal had been credited to that program. Forty-one percent of those dismissed had been hired by the Eisenhower Administration. Many were temporary employees or probationary employees. Not a single Communist had been uncovered by the program.

In 1956, seeking reelection as vice president, Nixon dropped the "security risk" scare story and the personal attacks on opponents. In place of it, he substituted a bland, upbeat standard speech which he delivered in whole or in part about two hundred times. It was as inane as his earlier speeches had been vicious. Reporters grew so weary of hearing it that for their own amusement, they devised code words for each section of the speech:

Rollercoaster: "I bring you good news. The Democratic campaign is on the downgrade and the Republican campaign is on the upgrade."

Weightlifter: "Dwight Eisenhower is a president you can hold up to your children as an example."

Thirty-two and Thirty-two: "In the past year, I have been in thirty-two countries and I can tell you America's prestige was never higher. In the past month, I have been in thirty-two states and I can tell you President Eisenhower was never more popular."

36

Stretch: "Now we have honest Eisenhower dollars instead of rubber Truman dollars."

Thirty Seconds: "Now I want to present the member of this campaign party who is doing more for our ticket . . ." This was the introduction of Mrs. Nixon, who stood, waved, and smiled. Since her introduction always came thirty seconds before the end of the speech, newspapermen used it as their signal to gather up their portable typewriters and dash for the press bus.

Even in that season of blandness, however, Nixon created a brief furor when he took partisan credit for the Supreme Court's school desegregation decision. It had, he said, been achieved under the leadership of "a great Republican Chief Justice, Earl Warren."

In 1958, he was again on the road for his party with a set speech in which he regularly announced, as if his personal assurance were needed, "there is only one party of treason—the Communist Party." Four years later in 1962, in his unsuccessful campaign for governor of California, he tried to make communism the prime issue in the campaign. The incumbent Democratic governor, Nixon contended, had failed to clamp down on subversive elements.

In 1968, Nixon ascended to power with the help of a widespread and well-contrived misunderstanding. He had previously espoused strongly hawkish views on the war and promised, in effect, to outperform President Johnson in achieving victory. But when Johnson on March 30 withdrew from the election race and initiated the Paris Peace Talks with the North Vietnamese, Nixon announced a self-imposed ban on further comment, ostensibly because he did not want domestic politics to intrude upon Johnson's peace negotiations. In reality, this self-denying ordinance enabled him to appear high-minded while he avoided disclosing that he had no plans for making peace but only a different strategy for waging war.

From April until his election in November, Nixon held few news conferences and avoided debate. His set speech was deliberately vague about Vietnam, promising opaquely "to end the war and win the peace." Many voters assumed that in some unexplained way he would negotiate with the Russians to bring pressure on the North Vietnamese and end the war within six months, the same period of time in which Eisenhower had ended the Korean stalemate. These voters would have been astonished if they knew that Nixon intended not to carry on Johnson's peace negotiations but to revive Johnson's discredited war policies and try the various military options Johnson had previously rejected.

Upon taking office, Nixon allowed the Paris talks to dwindle away into empty ritual. He kept the war going for another four and one-half years while another 20,000 American soldiers were killed, another 50,000 seriously wounded, and countless Asians died. He renewed the bombing and with far greater intensity than it had been carried out under Johnson. He extended the war by invading Cambodia. If Nixon had explained in advance that these were the actions he was prepared to take in Southeast Asia, he would not have been elected by the voters who naively assumed that they were choosing between two candidates both pledged to an early peaceful solution.

It was unfortunate enough that Nixon achieved office by a tacit deception of the public. But that deception had still other consequences. It meant that the war, the inflation, the unbalanced budgets, the demonstrations and turmoil in the streets would continue. There would be no relief for the disillusionment, no opportunity for a fresh start under the nation's new leadership. To persist in the management of an unpopular war meant that there would be a need for more dissimulation, more secrecy, more defiance of the Senate, more papering over of awkward facts by invoking the claims of "national security." The effect could only be a presidency under continued stress and the perpetuation of a siege mentality in the White House. Nixon, a hostile, withdrawn man, unsure of himself and deeply conflicted, would have been prone under the best of circumstances to indulge in conspiratorial thinking and to attempt to manipulate and control his political environment. But the circumstances of his taking power and his persistence in conducting an unpopular war hastened the drift toward a Watergate presidency.

What emerges from a study of Nixon's campaigns—of the personal vilification, the relentless negativism, the trumped-up issues, the canny silences and evasions, the flights from the press, the carefully shaded misstatements of other men's positions—is something more than the awkward shifts and tergiversations inevitable in a long political career. What emerges is a basic contempt for the democratic process. Nixon could not govern by persuasion and conciliation. He is a politician who is unaccustomed to stating the truth as he sees it and to defending his convictions in a frank exchange.

He is, as the London *Economist* once observed, "a true child of the age of propaganda." He is a marketer of images and a dealer in dreams. Every concept is reduced to its least common denominator, its slogan, its selling point. He has no allegiance to the truth, no commitment to any body of ideas, no interest in issues or social problems for their own sake. Truth, ideas, issues—these are markers to be used in the pursuit of personal power. Reactionary as his opinions about public policy are, they are of far less significance in his actions than the impulse to power. Thus he could urge American intervention to save the French in Vietnam in the spring of 1954 and take credit in the fall for Eisenhower's keeping the peace. He could denounce Stevenson's proposal for a unilateral American halt to nuclear testing as "catastrophic nonsense" in 1956 and praise Eisenhower's "initiative for peace" when he adopted the idea in 1958. He could denounce Stevenson for proposing to end the draft in 1956 and urge the same proposal himself in 1968. He could defend the Vietnam War in the winter of 1967-68 as "the cork in the bottle of Chinese expansionism" and upon taking office a year later immediately begin secret negotiations with the Chinese for a detente. He could spend twenty-five years denouncing price controls and then suddenly impose them in the summer of 1971.

Like an advertising man adapting his selling messages as he shifts from client to client, Nixon never stops writing messages for the buying public, but his client is always the same: himself. What changes are the tastes and fears and expectations of the public. In this agile, lifelong accommodation of himself and his messages, words and ideas dissolve into meaninglessness. What does it matter whether this or that is true if the people will buy it? Why be on the losing side of any issue if one can figure out a way to be on the winning side?

Of Nixon, it could be said as A. J. Balfour remarked of a British politician of his day: "His conscience is not his guide but his accomplice." In nearly thirty years in public life, Nixon pursued and exercised power in an ethical void. Watergate was born in that void. Having demonstrated in numerous campaigns that he has no faith in rational debate or in the power of ideas or in the capacity of ordinary citizens to understand complex matters, Nixon when he finally gained power naturally governed by secrecy and manipulation. He naturally yielded to the temptation to consolidate his power by force and fraud. He naturally retained the surplus from his 1968 campaign fund and used part of it to hire a detective to gather "dirt" on his political opponents. He naturally set up a secret police group in the White House to engage in burglaries, wiretaps, and other undercover missions. It was natural that ex-CIA agent E. Howard Hunt should be set to work doctoring State Department cables to make it appear that President Kennedy had personally ordered the murder of President Diem of South Vietnam. (Nixon was apparently willing to float a similar story personally. On September 16, 1971, at the very time that Hunt was phonying up the cables that were to be "leaked" to *Life* magazine, Nixon gratuitously observed at a news conference: "I would remind all concerned that the way we got into Vietnam in the first place was through overthrowing Diem, and the complicity in the murder of Diem.")

Nixon's lifetime of easy political lies and personal smears, of small discrepancies and specious doubletalk, led naturally to the sinister presidency, the secretly taped conversations in the Oval Office, the "enemy lists" and the criminal conspiracies, the hush money, the alleged promises of clemency, the perjured testimony, the obstruction of justice. A man who had lost, or perhaps never gained, a sense of political right and wrong on the road to power could never find that sense once power

40

was achieved. The White House does not change men. It magnifies their qualities, good and bad. But by their very nature, Richard Nixon's best qualities—intelligence, will, and industriousness—could not be barriers against his habits of chicanery and his bottomless cynicism. His success had to be as morally empty as the methods used to attain it. And so it was to be.

THE COMMITTEE

A Senate investigation is a uniquely American adventure in self-government. In any parliamentary country, a prime minister involved in a scandal of the magnitude and complexity of Watergate would have resigned. In Britain, a judge would have been appointed to investigate and submit a public report laying out all the facts. In a semi-presidential country such as France, DeGaulle or Pompidou might have fired his premier, called a snap referendum, or resigned and gone into disdainful retirement.

In America—where there is no tradition of presidents resigning, where separate branches of government share their powers with one another, and where the excutive is accountable to the people only at the next regularly scheduled election and to Congress only if it can find grounds to impeach him for "high crimes and misdemeanors"—great disputes of policy and great scandals are aired in prolonged Senate investigations.

A Senate investigation can serve many different purposes. It may help force the prosecutors to seek convictions: Senator Thomas R. Walsh's inquiry into Teapot Dome in the 1920's. It may produce valuable legislation: the investigation of stockmarket frauds by insiders that led to the Securities and Exchange Act of 1934. It may be pure theater: Senator Estes Kefauver's exciting but unproductive tour of the world of Frank Costello and the big-time gamblers. It may expose injustice: Senator Robert M. LaFollette's study of anti-labor violence in the 1930's and the Senate Rackets Committee inquiry into union gangsterism and corruption in the 1950's. It may speed the downfall of a demagogue: the Army-McCarthy hearings in 1954. It may develop and rehearse the issues in a great matter of public policy but leave them unresolved: the inquiry into General MacArthur's firing in 1951.

No investigation was ever more momentous in its implications than the investigation into the Watergate scandals that the Senate authorized on February 7, 1973, when it established the Select Committee on Presidential Campaign Activities and ordered it to

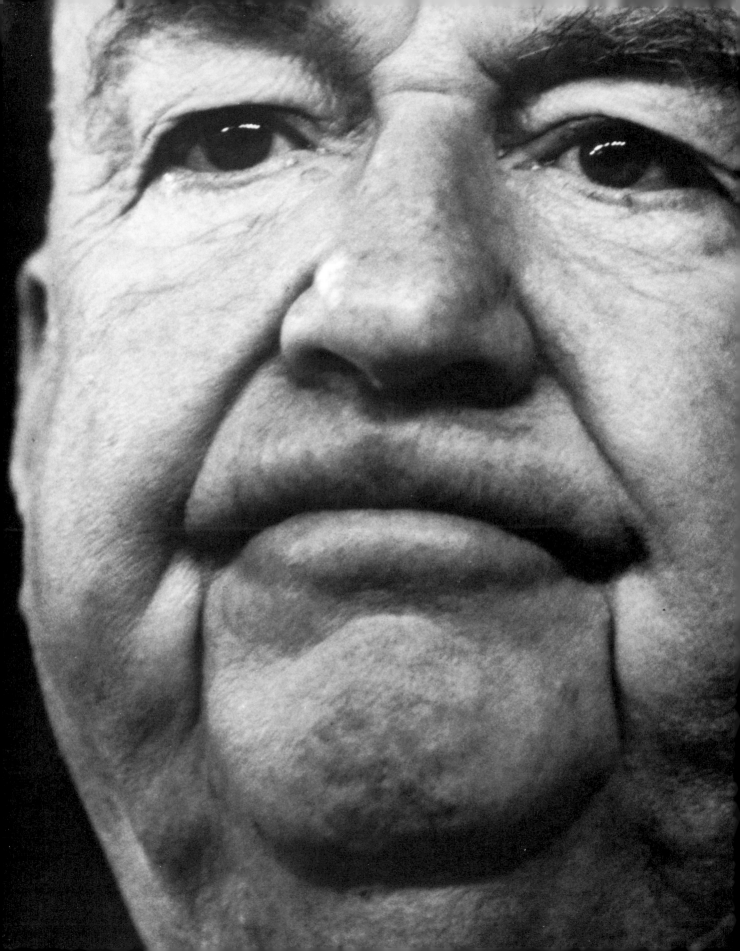

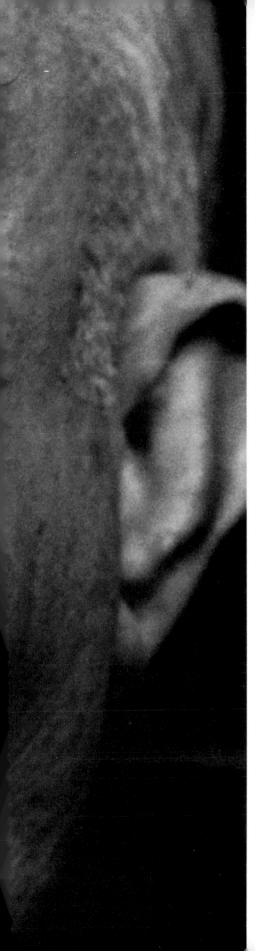

report within one year on "the extent, if any, to which illegal, improper, or unethical activities were engaged in by any persons, acting either individually or in combination with others, in the presidential election of 1972, or in any related campaign or canvass conducted by or in behalf of any person seeking nomination or election as the candidate of any political party for the office of President of the United States in such election, and to determine whether in its judgment any occurrences which may be revealed by the investigation and study indicate the necessity or desirability of the enactment of new congressional legislation to safeguard the electoral process by which the President of the United States is chosen."

Never before had a Senate committee been given a mandate to determine for the public's satisfaction the lawfulness and moral legitimacy of the means used by an incumbent president to retain power and to exercise that power.

Despite the solemnity of the issues, a Senate investigating committee's public hearings are not a solemn affair. They are a mixture of legislative fact-finding and rambling debate, of grand jury and trial court, of morality play and comedy hour. They can be stupefying in their dullness and startling in their dramatic intensity.

Notwithstanding the many previous investigations, each major inquiry works out its own rules, evolves its own methods of approaching its special task, and takes on a distinctive personality. The committee chairman, the ranking minority member, and the chief counsel are the decisive persons in shaping a committee's performance. So it was with the Watergate Committee.

In accord with Senate custom, Senator Sam J. Ervin, Jr., North Carolina Democrat, became chairman because he was author of the resolution proposing the investigation. At seventy-six, he was the third oldest man in the Senate, a veteran of eighteen years' service, respected by both parties. During his first decade in the Senate, Ervin was best known in Washington for his pivotal role in the Southern filibusters against the successive civil rights bills of the late 1950's and early 1960's. Richard B. Russell of Georgia was the leader and chief strategist of the Southern bloc, and Ervin was the legal brains. Hour after hour he held the floor, patiently, doggedly, good-humoredly, making constitutional arguments against federal civil rights legislation on the grounds that it would infringe the rights of the individuals and of the states. It was a morally doomed cause that stretched back to John C. Calhoun, and Ervin was the last of many good men to serve it. A graduate of the University of North Carolina and of Harvard Law School, he brought to this losing struggle more than thirty years of experience as a trial lawyer, state legislator, Congressman (for part of one term), and state judge. He had served eight years as a judge in lower courts and six on the state supreme court.

Although he sometimes became emotionally wrought-up in those debates, he did so in that professional way that trial lawyers become involved in heated courtroom arguments. He never lost his innate Southern courtesy or stooped to racist demagoguery or personal bitterness. He interspersed his constitutional arguments with the rural Southern anecdotes, biblical quotations, and bits of homely philosophy that in 1973 were to become so familiar to millions of television viewers. Liberals

in the Senate came to respect him as a worthy and
formidable antagonist, while his work in those battles
gave him solid personal standing with the Southern
Democrats and Goldwater Republicans.

Unlike President Nixon, who calls himself
a strict constructionist but stretches the law to fit his
needs, Ervin really is a fundamentalist about the
Constitution and believes in interpreting its language
in a strict, even literal, sense. This approach impels him
to certain libertarian convictions about the rights of
individual citizens and the limits of government. As
the controversy over civil rights faded away, Senator Ervin
increasingly involved himself in legislative battles
concerning the use of Army Intelligence to spy upon
civilians, the extent of a newsman's right to protect his
sources in a grand jury criminal investigation, the
President's claim of "executive privilege" to withhold
from Congress information and the testimony of his
subordinates, and the President's power arbitrarily to
"impound" money appropriated by Congress. When
the Watergate burglary led to widespread reports of
political espionage and sabotage and of criminal
conspiracy to conceal them, this doughty old
constitutionalist reacted strongly. What could be more
subversive of America than to interfere with the citizens'
free choice of their elected officials and then to lie about
it to the grand jury and the courts? These sinister crimes
and conspiracies had to be investigated and the facts
made plain to the American people as a cautionary tale.
In the Indian Summer of his days, Ervin had found the
historic service to this republic that he was uniquely
qualified to perform.

It was as if his whole life had prepared Sam

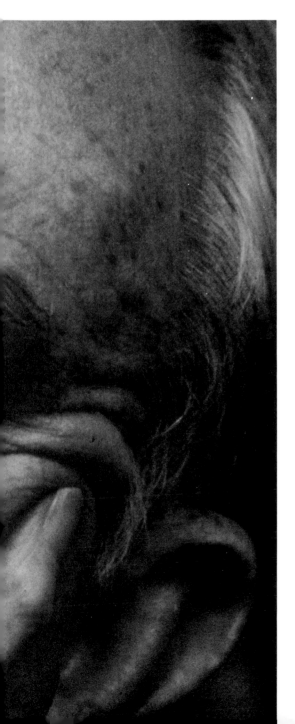

Ervin for his task as chairman of the Senate Watergate Committee. Ervin is a man of narrow but deep experience. As a youth of twenty-one in World War I, he served in France with the First Division, was twice wounded in battle, twice cited for gallantry in action, and awarded the Purple Heart with Oak Leaf Cluster, the Silver Star, and the Distinguished Service Cross. He has always lived in the small town of Morganton, North Carolina (population 13,615), where he was born. He and his wife have lived in the same house for half a century. In Washington, they occupy a small apartment in the Methodist Building, one block from the Senate Office Building and favored by many Capitol Hill employees because it has a dining room that serves plain, inexpensive food. In eighteen years in the Senate, he has taken only two extended vacations. He has always worshiped in Morganton's First Presbyterian Church, participated in the rites of the Masonic Order (past Grand Orator of North Carolina's Grand Lodge), and twice served as trustee of his alma mater. In a time when increasing numbers of Americans feel rootless and morally confused, Ervin is a man who knows where he came from and who he is. He brought to bear a firm, unwavering moral perspective upon the tangled crimes, deceits, evasions, and rationalizations of Watergate. With his beautifully gnarled hands rapping the gavel carved for him by a North Carolina Cherokee Indian and with his eyebrows waggling, his jowls aquiver, and his voice sometimes stammering as his thoughts rushed ahead of his words, Ervin embodied and bespoke the conscience of the nation. In a society that worships youth, he proved the soundness of Plato's view that nothing beats a wise old man.

The other Democratic members of the Committee were chosen by a curious process of elimination. A Senate aide familiar with the thinking of Senator Mike Mansfield, the majority leader, explained it this way: "First, he eliminated the freshmen. Then he eliminated the past and potential presidential candidates—McGovern, Humphrey, Muskie, Kennedy, Mondale, Bayh, and Jackson—because he was afraid they would give the committee a partisan image. He was trying to counter the Republican argument that the whole investigation was a political scalping raid from the outset. Once he had set those ground rules, there were not too many Democrats to choose from."

Some Democrats grumbled privately that this approach was typical of Mansfield's flaccid leadership. The Republicans, they pointed out, had imposed no such self-denying ordnance on themselves. They had not matched Ervin by selecting their own oldest and most senior member, George Aiken of Vermont. Instead, they had chosen as their top man on the committee Howard H. Baker of Tennessee, youthful-looking, telegenic, politically ambitious.

There seemed no good reason for the Democrats to have eliminated from consideration their attractive freshmen members such as William Hathaway of Maine, Richard Clark of Iowa, and James Abourezk of South Dakota. Even by Mansfield's own ground rules, he could have selected senior members who would have brought enthusiasm to the assignment and an intellectual cutting edge to their questions, men such as Thomas Eagleton of Missouri, Adlai E. Stevenson of Illinois, Gaylord Nelson of Wisconsin, Harold Hughes of Iowa, and John V. Tunney of California.

As it was, the Democrats placed on the Com-

52

54

mittee three of their least well-known and rather atypical members, Herman E. Talmadge of Georgia, Daniel K. Inouye of Hawaii, and Joseph M. Montoya of New Mexico.

Talmadge is one of the shrewdest men in the Senate, as his sometimes astute questioning of witnesses demonstrated, but he regarded the Committee only as a chore to be tolerated. When Mansfield first asked him to serve, he refused.

"I told him I had more pressing business, but he said he wanted me. When you're asked like that by the leadership, you pretty much go along," he said.

Talmadge, who celebrated his sixtieth birthday August 7, 1973, the day the Watergate Committee recessed its first round of hearings, is the son of "Ole Gene" Talmadge, the gallus-snapping, Negro-baiting populist demagogue who was several times Governor of Georgia. Herman, too, served as Governor for six years from 1949 to 1955. Two years later, he succeeded the veteran Walter George in the Senate and is now completing his third term.

Like many men who are sons of colorful fathers, Talmadge has developed a wholly different style. He shuns controversy when he can, makes no rabble-rousing speeches, and has developed a solid network of allies in the business community without losing touch with his father's political base among the small farmers. As chairman of the Agriculture Committee and ranking member of the tax-writing Finance Committee, he is in a position to protect the interests of both his farmer and business constituents. He speaks infrequently on the floor of the Senate and has no interest in the national publicity that his membership on the Watergate Committee has brought him. Within the power structure of the Senate, however,

55

he is one of the influential insiders. On many substantive domestic and foreign policy issues, he is as often allied with the Nixon Administration as with the leadership of his own party.

Talmadge did no homework to prepare for each day's hearings. He relied on a few staff-prepared questions and his own quick intelligence in asking his questions.

"I see myself as a juror," he said, "and a juror doesn't background himself."

Joseph M. Montoya, fifty-eight, is a career politician and a member of one of the dozen interrelated families that dominate the Spanish American wing of the Democratic Party in New Mexico. He was elected to the lower house of the state legislature in 1936 when he was only twenty-one and still attending Georgetown University Law School in Washington, D.C. After more than twenty years in the state legislature and as Lieutenant Governor, he was elected to the House of Representatives in a special election in 1957 and moved up to the Senate in 1964. As Texans and other "Anglos" have moved into the state in increasing numbers in recent years, New Mexico's politics have become increasingly conservative, and Montoya's old-line Democratic faction weakened. He was reelected with only 52 percent of the vote in 1970 after a hard campaign. He has a liberal record on domestic issues and was an early opponent of the Vietnam War.

56

Senator Montoya

He is the epitome of the colorless "constituents' Senator" who busies himself mostly with the problems of his state.

Montoya's questions were often repetitive and loosely phrased. As former White House counsel John W. Dean III concluded a devastating opening statement that indicted President Nixon and a dozen of his top aides, an anonymous note passed up and down the press tables. It read: "Montoya's first question when his time comes: 'Mister Dean, what was your position at the White House?'"

Actually, his first question was not quite that bad. It was: "Mr. Dean, you mentioned in yesterday's testimony about the briefings that were being given to Mr. Ziegler prior to his making public statements with respect to this situation involving the break-in at the Watergate. Now, will you please give me a little more information as to the intensity or the extent of these briefings?"

Next to Ervin, the most effective questioner on the majority side of the committee was Senator Inouye. With his impassive countenance, unblinking stare, and almost dead-level voice, he reminded television viewers of actor Peter Lorre.

Descended from Japanese immigrants long resident in Hawaii, Inouye enlisted at eighteen in the 442nd Regimental Combat Team that was made up of Nisei and compiled a famous record during World War II. He received a battlefield commission of second lieutenant and lost his right arm in combat.

58

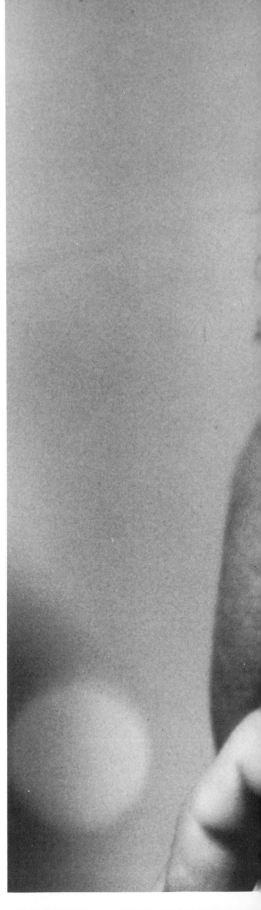

Senator Inouye

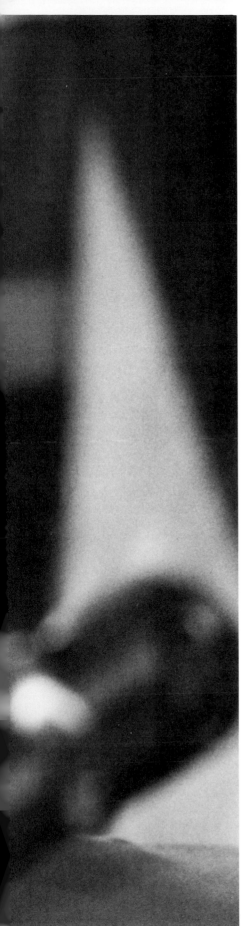

After the war, he graduated from the University of Hawaii and George Washington University Law School in Washington, D.C. Two years out of law school, he was elected to the territorial legislature. When Hawaii gained statehood in 1959, he became one of the state's first two Congressmen, moving up to the Senate three years later.

Inouye is Hawaii's most powerful and popular politician, winning a second term in the Senate in 1968 with 83 percent of the vote.

On the Republican side, Howard H. Baker was the first choice of his wily rival, Senator Hugh Scott of Pennsylvania, to be the senior Republican on the Committee. With tacit White House approval, Baker has twice run against Scott for the post of minority floor leader and twice narrowly lost. In those battles, Baker had the support of conservative Republicans of the Barry Goldwater-Strom Thurmond-Roman Hruska variety while Scott was favored by the liberal and middle-of-the-road Republicans. In choosing Baker for a spot where he could gain advantageous national publicity, Scott was conciliating a dangerous antagonist and doing the best he could for the White House in a difficult situation.

Baker is a long-time personal friend and political ally of President Nixon. Like Nixon, he is fundamentally conservative but not stodgily so. He has broken out of the right-wing mold on certain issues such as mass transit and protection of the environment. Characteristically, Baker had a private meeting with the President when the investigation was getting started to work out a line of cooperation between himself and the White House. Without committing himself to any whitewash, Baker was prepared to help the President make his case. As events

61

developed, however, the President's Watergate difficulties proved more complex and far-ranging than Baker had anticipated, while the President, for his part, apparently did not feel he could take the Senator fully into his confidence. Baker helped Nixon as much as he felt he could, but no one could help him enough.

Baker is a member of an unusual political family. His father was a member of the House for thirteen years. When he died, Baker's stepmother filled out his unexpired term. Baker's wife, Joy, is a daughter of Everett McKinley Dirksen, the late Senate Republican leader. His sister May is married to William C. Wampler, a Virginia Republican Congressman.

Baker comes from eastern Tennessee, the traditional Republican stronghold in the state. His first political race was for the U.S. Senate in 1964. He was swept under by the anti-Goldwater tide, but two years later ran again and won. He was easily reelected in 1972.

Edward J. Gurney of Florida was "the company man" on the Committee. Although he made considerable show of serious concern, there was never any doubt that he was in there doing his best to defend Richard Nixon's interests at all times. That was not because he was personally close to the President but, paradoxically, because he was not close enough. Nixon's long-time ally in Florida Republican politics is former Congressman William Cramer. Bill Cramer served sixteen years from the St. Petersburg district. He passed up the chance to run for the Senate in 1968 because he did not want to risk his safe seat. Gurney, a much more junior figure in the House, ran and won. Two years later, Cramer finally made his move for the Senate and was defeated in a major upset by "Walking Lawton" Chiles, the Democrat who started

63

the fad of walking across a state to seek votes. Gurney's
concern was that Cramer might run against him in the
1974 Senatorial primary with White House backing.
To try to ward off that possibility and neutralize potential
White House disaffection, Gurney, already a staunch
right-winger, established himself as a Nixon superloyalist.

Gurney first became highly visible in that role in
the spring of 1972 when the Senate Judiciary Committee's
hearings on the nomination of Richard Kleindienst as
Attorney General turned into an unsuccessful attempt to
investigate the Administration's questionable settlement
of an antitrust suit against ITT, the giant conglomerate.
Gurney freely acknowledges fronting for the Administration in the fight to head off a complete investigation.

"It was such a highly partisan investigation,"
he said. "Someone had to play the role of defending the
President, and I did."

Gurney in the Watergate investigation raised
the cry early and often that the hearings were taking too
much time and that the whole inquiry should be rushed
to a conclusion. In late July 1973, before John Ehrlichman
and H. R. Haldeman had even testified, Gurney was
complaining that "the hearings are damaging this country
seriously and our relations with nations abroad."

Lean, handsome, and well tailored, Gurney,
sixty, is a native of Maine who moved to Winter Park,
Florida, after World War II. He practiced law and engaged
in local politics until elected to the House in 1962.

Lowell P. Weicker, Jr., of Connecticut is, at
six feet, six inches and 250 pounds, physically the biggest
man in the Senate. Morally and politically, he grew to
increased stature during the Watergate hearings. Weicker
has the instinctive self-confidence of an individual born

64

to great wealth and social position. An heir to the Squibb pharmaceutical fortune, he was born in Paris in 1931 where his parents were temporarily resident. He is a graduate of the Lawrenceville School and Yale, class of '53, spent two years in the Army, and then graduated from the University of Virginia Law School.

"I'm a professional politician," Weicker likes to say. He entered elective politics almost immediately after law school, serving in the Connecticut legislature and as First Selectman (mayor) of Greenwich, a posh exurban town. He won a seat in the House in 1968 from Fairfield County, the wealthy, sprawling district where many New York City commuters live. Two years later he was elected to the Senate.

Weicker has great gusto for life, loves music, is a gourmet cook and likes to eat, and plays an energetic if erratic game of tennis.

He responded early to the challenge of Watergate, asked the leadership for a place on the Committee, and with the help of additional private staff, paid for out of his own pocket, he quickly confirmed on his own that top White House insiders had run the Watergate cover-up. In March 1973 he publicly called for Haldeman's resignation.

Weicker's indignation at the chicanery and ruthlessness exposed in the hearings sometimes caused his words to come spluttering out slower than his mind and emotions moved. But the genuineness of his convictions came through clearly. In one of his striking extemporaneous outbursts at the White House's dirty tricks, he exclaimed: "Republicans don't cover up, don't reject their fellow Americans as enemies to be harassed, but as human beings to be loved and wanted."

66

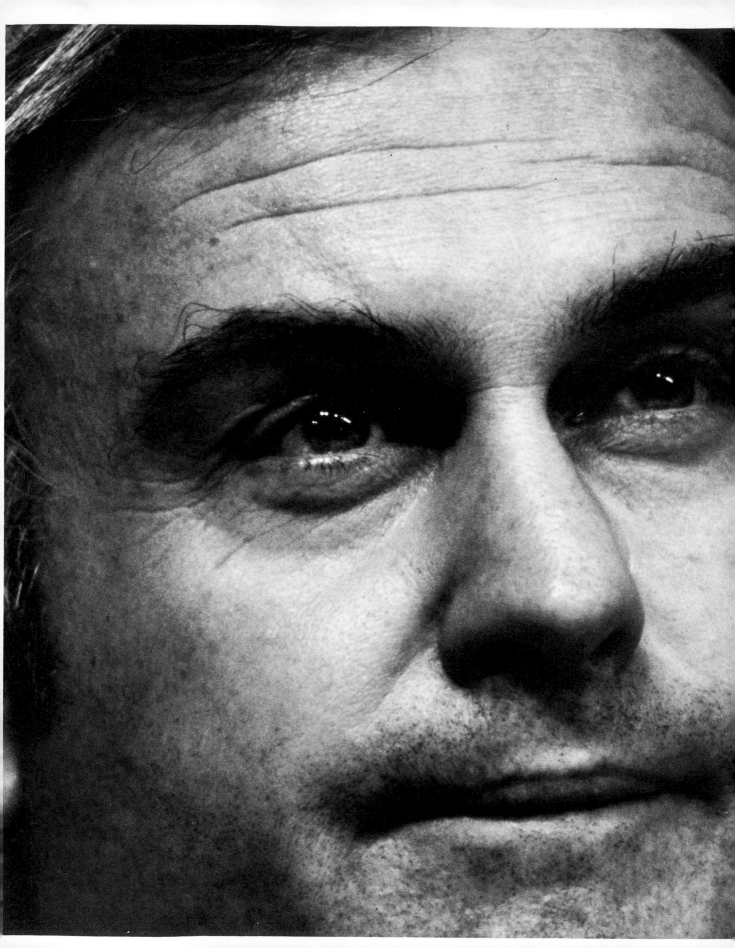

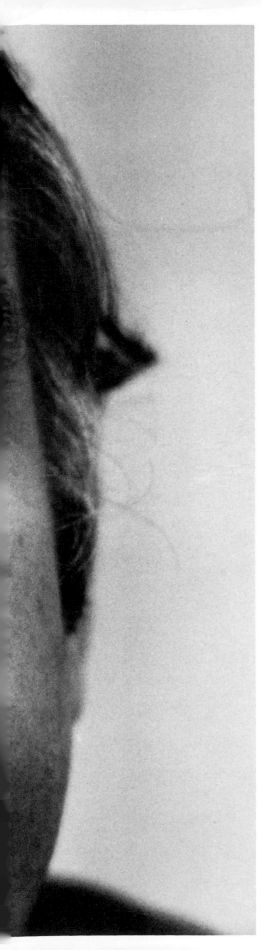

It was Weicker who alone was able to puncture Haldeman's bland, cool exterior by cross-examining him about a memorandum in which he wrote "good" in the margin alongside a forecast of violent, obscene demonstrations against Nixon. Haldeman had a hard time explaining that comment.

It was Weicker who dueled with John Ehrlichman over the latter's hiring of Tony Ulasewicz, a retired New York City detective, to dig up "dirt" about the private lives of Administration critics and political opponents. "You definitely have two concepts of politics in this country meeting head on," Weicker said. "You stick to your version, I am going to stick to mine."

Ulasewicz, who testified on two different occasions before the Committee, was scheduled to be recalled for a third appearance to discuss the investigations he had conducted and the "dirt" he had dug up on leading Democrats. But behind the scenes, Weicker protested vehemently to his colleagues that Ulasewicz with his droll manner and wise-cracking comments was making a comedy out of a serious enterprise. At his insistence, Ulasewicz was not recalled.

Having befriended L. Patrick Gray III, the former acting director of the FBI, Weicker brought out the

69

Senator Weicker

full poignance of Gray's betrayal by the White House.

When the four Cuban exiles who had carried out the Watergate burglaries and been sentenced to prison decided to seek counsel about their plight, they asked Weicker to come visit them. He took down their account during an hour-long visit in the Federal prison at Danbury, Connecticut. Before leaving, he told them again: "I still don't know why you fellows chose me to talk to. I have no influence at the White House. I can't get you clemency."

Eugenio Martinez, the most articulate and probably the most intelligent of the burglars, said: "Ah, Senator, we watched on television. We wanted to talk to you because you would understand us. You are the only romantic on the Committee!"

Senators, like generals, often re-fight the previous war. Chairman Sam Ervin was determined that his inquiry would be quite different from the most notorious Senate investigation of his time, the raucous and inconsequent inquisition run by Joe McCarthy and his reckless young counsel, Roy Cohn. In Samuel Dash, professor at George-town University Law School and director of its Institute for Criminal Law and Procedure, Ervin found for the job of chief counsel an experienced lawyer totally unlike the brash, hectoring, self-centered Cohn.

Dash, forty-eight, is a low-keyed, careful, scholarly liberal with impressive professional credentials and abundant experience. He is a past chairman of the criminal law section of the American Bar Association, a past president of the National Association of Defense Lawyers in Criminal Cases, and is chairman of the Public

70

Defender Service for Washington, D.C. The son of
Russian Jewish immigrants, Dash was born in Camden,
New Jersey, worked his way through Temple University
and Harvard Law School, began as a trial attorney for the
Criminal Division of the Department of Justice, joined
the staff of the District Attorney in Philadelphia, and at
age thirty in 1955, when the top job fell vacant, became
District Attorney. He served for eighteen months. Because
he found the pressures of a big-city prosecutor's life
uncongenial, Dash did not seek election in his own right,
turning away toward a quieter career of writing, teaching,
and private practice. He did a study on wiretapping for
the Pennsylvania Bar Association that grew into his book,
The Eavesdroppers, the standard work on the subject.
Dash, a fluent and skilled writer who composes verse for
family celebrations, was once asked by the late Erle Stanley
Gardner to join the staff of writers who "fleshed out"
the plots that Gardner dreamed up for his mystery novels.
Marlon Brando, who had bought the film rights to Carol
Chessman's life story, engaged Dash to review Chessman's
criminal career and suggest a screenplay. Dash proposed
a plot about a law professor who investigates Chessman's
life with the story to be told in flashbacks. The project
came to nothing.

    "I spent a whole day with Brando going over it,
and by the end of the day," Dash recalls, "Brando decided
he didn't want to play Chessman. He wanted to play the
law professor."

    Or as Mrs. Dash prefers to tell it: "In those
days, I used to joke that Marlon Brando really wanted to
play Sam Dash."

    Dash's work as an expert on electronic sur-
veillance and the legal problems connected with it brought

Majority counsel Samuel Dash

73

him to Ervin's attention. Dash had been a witness before the Senate Subcommittee on Constitutional Rights chaired by Ervin. His expertise also evoked the Nixon Administration's surly attentions. In a speech to a convention of the American Bar Association, Dash attacked Attorney General John Mitchell's contention that the Justice Department could wiretap without court authority in internal security cases. The Law Enforcement Assistance Administration, an agency of the Justice Department that finances research in crime control, soon afterward informed the National Association of Attorneys General that it would get no further research funds as long as Dash was a part-time paid consultant. When Dash dropped off the payroll and became a volunteer, the group obtained its funds. After Dash became director of the institute at Georgetown, the LEAA stopped funding it.

Minority counsel Fred D. Thompson

"I had only three stipulations when Senator Ervin offered me the job. I told him I wanted to be completely independent; that I would take the facts as far as they would go; and I would hire my own staff. And Senator Ervin said: 'I'll put that in writing, and even if I go back on my word, you can hold me to it.'"

It was put in writing, but neither man ever had to look at the contract again.

The deputy counsel of the Committee was Rufus Edmisten, a young North Carolinian who has worked for Ervin for almost a decade. Tall, full-faced, and often smiling, Edmisten appears in many photographs since he sat immediately behind Ervin. He is his most trusted aide.

Dash selected three assistant chief counsels: David Dorsen, who had been deputy head of New York City's Department of Investigation; Terry Lenzner, a

former assistant U.S. Attorney in New York who had served briefly in the Nixon Administration as head of the Anti-Poverty Program's Legal Services and quit in anger; and James Hamilton, a trial attorney for the big Washington firm of Covington and Burling. For the job as the committee's chief investigator, Dash hired the legendary Carmine Bellino, an FBI agent who has worked for congressional investigations for a quarter-century, most notably under Robert Kennedy in the Senate Rackets Committee's investigation of James Hoffa and the Teamsters Union.

As part of the bipartisan arrangement establishing the Committee, the Republicans were given control of one-third of the staff. Senator Baker chose a fellow Tennessean, Fred D. Thompson, as Chief Minority Counsel. Thompson, only thirty, had several years' experience prosecuting bank robbers and moonshiners as an Assistant U.S. Attorney in Nashville, but this was his debut in the big time. His assignment was anomalous since there is not a "majority" or "minority" way to investigate crimes and conspiracies. In effect, Thompson and his aides served as a check on Dash's staff to make certain that they were not unfair to the Administration witnesses in developing the facts. With his sideburns, colorful shirts, and slow Southern speech, Thompson became a distinctive television personality.

THE WITNESSES

COPS AND ROBBERS

The public downfall of a lawless presidency began with a bungled burglary. The Senate Watergate Committee, after taking testimony from two preliminary witnesses, began its public hearings by focusing on that burglary and its immediate consequences.

Sergeant Paul W. Leeper of the Washington Police Department told of receiving a call on his car radio at 1:52 A.M. on June 17, 1972, to investigate a possible burglary at the Watergate. He and officers John Barrett and Carl Shoffler are detectives who, casually dressed and driving an unmarked car, cruise high-crime areas. Normally, a regular squad car with uniformed police would have responded to a routine call from the nightwatchman at the Watergate. But the nearest squad car had stopped for gas and the call was relayed to the detectives who happened to be nearby. Their tour of duty ended at midnight, but to earn overtime pay they had volunteered for extra duty.

Arriving at the Watergate, they attracted no attention in their plainclothes from Alfred C. Baldwin III, the ex-FBI agent acting as a lookout for the burglars from his post on a balcony of the Howard Johnson Motel across the street. Inside the Democratic National Committee's headquarters on the sixth floor of the Watergate were four exiles from Cuba, headed by Bernard L. Barker. With them was James McCord, security coordinator for the Committee to Reelect the President, who, as an expert on electronic eavesdropping, had accompanied them to install additional telephone taps—a minor art he was to demonstrate for the Senate Watergate Committee and millions of television viewers a year later. In Room 214 of the hotel wing of the Watergate complex were the masterminds of the evening's operation, E. Howard Hunt

79

Sergeant Paul W. Leeper

from the White House and G. Gordon Liddy from the Committee to Reelect the President.

The detectives began their routine search of the building on the eighth floor. When the lights came on there, Baldwin alerted Barker.

"O.K., we know about that," Barker replied on his walkie-talkie. "That's the two o'clock guard check. Let us know if lights go on any other place."

A few minutes later, the detectives moved down to the sixth floor and went out to search the balcony. Baldwin then radioed Hunt.

"Are our people dressed in suits or dressed casually?" he inquired.

"What?" asked Hunt.

When Baldwin repeated the question, Hunt said, "Our people are dressed in suits."

"Well, we've got problems," replied Baldwin. "We've got some people dressed casually and they've got guns. They're looking around the balcony and everywhere but they haven't come across our people."

Hunt then tried to contact his burglars, but Barker had thriftily turned off his walkie-talkie to save its batteries. Unwarned, they were arrested moments later by Sergeant Leeper and his partners.

They surrendered meekly. Sergeant Leeper told the Watergate Committee that they "were five of the easiest lock-ups I ever had."

Hunt and Liddy rushed from their hotel room to their car. While Liddy waited in the car, Hunt went to Baldwin's room in the Howard Johnson Motel and told him to gather up all the electronic eavesdropping equipment and clear out. Baldwin, who had been looking forward to his trip to Miami Beach, where more wire-

80

Police officer Carl Shoffler

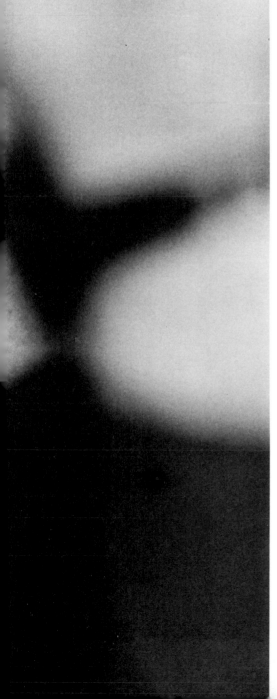

tapping was planned at the Democratic National Convention, called to Hunt as he disappeared down the hall: "Does this mean I won't be going to Miami?"

Detective-story fans will always ponder the chain of circumstances that pried open the Watergate mystery. If an ordinary police car had responded to the Watergate call, Baldwin, the lookout, would have sounded a warning in time for the others to escape. If Barker had not switched off his walkie-talkie, they might still have been able to get away. Why did McCord tape the garage door after Vergilio Gonzalez, the locksmith in the burglary group, had successfully picked the lock? The tape alerted the suspicions of the nightwatchman, but it was not essential to ensure the burglars' escape. And why were the burglars neatly dressed as businessmen? Why were they not disguised as workmen—plumbers, perhaps— making emergency repairs in the Democratic offices? Or, alternatively, if dressed in business suits, why did they not turn on all the lights, set one of their number to running the mimeograph machine, and pretend to be legitimate Democratic Party volunteers?

After the five men were seized at the Watergate, the police and the FBI soon obtained enough evidence to pick up Liddy and Hunt. The grand jury indicted these seven on September 15. When the case went to trial before Judge John J. Sirica in January 1973, Hunt and the four Cuban exiles followed the White House scenario and pleaded guilty. Liddy and McCord, for quite different reasons, pleaded innocent. Baldwin, the lookout, became a witness for the government and escaped prosecution.

Jeb Stuart Magruder, the deputy campaign manager, perjured himself and testified that he knew

James W. McCord, Jr.

nothing of the burglaries and wiretapping. His subordinates, he testified, had gone off half-cocked on their own. Judge Sirica repeatedly took over the questioning of the witnesses, and expressed open scepticism about their story. After the jury found the defendants guilty, Judge Sirica meted out long prison terms to all except McCord, who by then had agreed to tell all that he knew.

The committee heard testimony from only three of the seven Watergate burglars: Barker, McCord, and Hunt. Liddy made it plain in a staff interview that he would refuse to testify. Since the four Cubans were so clearly Hunt's dupes, only Barker, their straw boss, was asked to testify. In earnest, bumbling fashion, Barker made it plain that personal loyalty and not political thought is his strong point. "It was not my job to think," he said.

The sensational witness in the opening days was McCord, the silent Oklahoman, thin-lipped, strong-featured, and wholly self-possessed. Aside from brief stints in the FBI and the Army Air Force, he had spent his adult career in the CIA. A flawless organization man who took orders and respected channels of authority, McCord was deeply devoted to "the company,"as CIA old-timers call the agency. After he had retired in 1970, a friend, John Caulfield, the former New York City detective on the White House staff, recommended him for the job of security coordinator at the Committee to Reelect the President. Asked why he was drawn into clandestine and illegal political operations, McCord told the Committee he thought the Administration had given them the color of legality. "There were several motivations, but one of the basic motivations was the fact that this

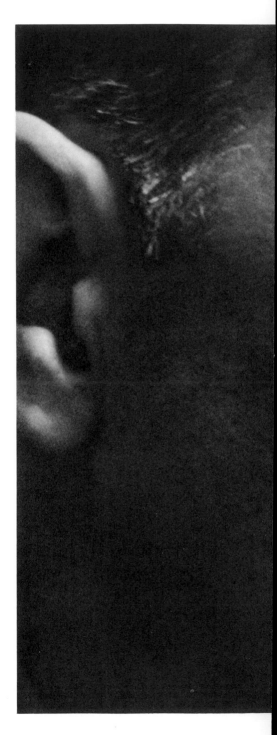

Alfred C. Baldwin III

man, the Attorney General [John Mitchell], had approved it in his offices at a series of meetings in which he had obviously given careful consideration to it, while he was the top legal officer of the United States Government, and that the counsel to the President had sat in with him [Mitchell] during such discussions."

McCord, a devoted family man and a church-going Methodist—and now on trial—had no intention of going to prison while those higher in authority stayed free and assumed no responsibility. A society-page photograph of Jeb Stuart Magruder, the deputy chief of the Committee to Reelect the President, who was now director of Nixon's Second Inaugural festivities, particularly irritated McCord. More fundamental was his fear that the White House was trying to put the blame for Watergate on the CIA.

McCord and Caulfield corroborated one another's accounts of how the White House reacted to the danger that McCord might defect. Early in January 1973, as the Watergate trial was getting underway, John Dean, counsel to the President, telephoned Caulfield and asked him to pass a message to McCord. Caulfield, realizing that he was getting involved in the obstruction of justice, used Anthony Ulasewicz as an intermediary. Ulasewicz telephoned McCord at his home and told him to go to Route 355 and position himself in a pay phone booth near the Blue Fountain Inn.

Bernard L. Barker

McCord did so and heard Ulasewicz, whose identity was unknown to him, read the message that Dean had transmitted through Caulfield: "Plead guilty. One year is a long time. You will get executive clemency. Your family will be taken care of and when you get out you will be rehabilitated and a job will be found for you."

"One year is a long time" meant that a year is a long enough time for the public to forget, but it is also a long time to be incarcerated in prison. McCord refused to commit himself. There followed three meetings between him and Caulfield at the second overlook of the George Washington Parkway on the Virginia side of the Potomac. On Dean's instructions, Caulfield told McCord that the promise of future clemency "comes from the very highest levels of the White House." McCord restated Caulfield's argument to the Committee in his own terse fashion: "The President's ability to govern is at stake. Another Teapot Dome scandal is possible, and the government may fall. Everybody is on track but you. You are not following the game plan. Get closer to your attorney. You seem to be pursuing your own course of action."

McCord, inner-directed and self-contained, had charted his own course. He pleaded innocent, volunteered nothing during the trial, and was found guilty. Then on March 23, the day the defendants were to be sentenced, Judge John Sirica read in open court a letter from McCord asserting that there had been "political pressures" on the defendants to plead guilty, that perjury had been committed at the trial, and that unnamed, more powerful persons were involved.

The first Watergate cover-up had been blown apart.

John J. Caulfield

THE SAD YOUNG MEN

They were Richard Nixon's children, those sad young men who came day by day before the Watergate Committee. They told their stories of files neatly kept, of "talking papers" and "action papers," of trips in *Air Force One* and messages relayed on "secure" telephones, and of their gradual participation in crime. The end all came so suddenly, so unexpectedly. In a few, swift, unraveling months, they had moved from the hushed corridors of power to the strained recollections of the grand jury room and the frantic bargaining for immunity.

It used to be thought that it was the Kennedy Administration that brought young men to power in Washington. But the Nixon Administration far exceeded any of its predecessors in putting young men in high places. Consider their ages: John Dean, 34; Fred Fielding, 34; Egil Krogh, 33; Gordon Strachan, 30; Bruce Kehrli, 28; Hugh Sloan, 32; Robert Odle, 29; Robert Reisner, 26; Dwight Chapin, 32. And those were their ages in the spring of 1973 when the Watergate hearings began, making even more remarkable their appointments three or four years earlier. For several of them, their jobs in the White House or in the Nixon campaign organization were the first jobs of any consequence they had ever held.

Except for one or two who had the good sense to pull back from personal involvement at the last moment, they either turned blind eyes to the wickedness going on around them or willingly participated in perjury, burglary, and destruction of evidence. Why were they all so susceptible? Why did so few of them show any moral independence or backbone? Why did Nixon and his senior staff surround themselves with these much younger and unqualified aides?

One could reasonably conclude from the Watergate fiasco that only older, more experienced men should be appointed even to middle-level jobs in the White House. But that would be a generational slur on many able young people in their twenties and thirties. The young men who worked for Richard Nixon were not the best talent of their generation. They were not prodigies, not first in their class or editors

91

Gordon C. Strachan

Robert C. Odle, Jr.

of law reviews or authors of promising books.

It is easy to understand why the two senior
men on the staff—H. R. Haldeman, 46, and John D.
Ehrlichman, 48—wanted traditionally important White
House posts such as appointments secretary, press
secretary, and legal counsel occupied by callow,
inexperienced men. As power monopolists, whose own
prior experience in politics was thin and in government
nonexistent, Haldeman and Ehrlichman did not want
anyone around of comparable age or greater experience
who might challenge their supremacy. Moreover, an older
man might not have stood for the bullying that Haldeman
inflicted on Gordon Strachan, his political deputy,
bawling him out in a 4 A.M. telephone call and requiring
him to wear a "beeper" so that his whereabouts would
never be in doubt. Finally, both senior men were familiar
from earlier Nixon campaigns with political "dirty
tricks," and had to find aides prepared to accommodate
themselves to the chosen methods of their superiors. It
was no accident that there were so many willing
accomplices on the staff before and after the crime
of Watergate.

The young men they selected came from

93

Bruce A. Kehrli

comfortable backgrounds. A few of them came from wealthy families. They were socially poised, members of the "right" fraternities, successful campus politicians, and big men on campus. They were gentlemen athletes, swimmers and tennis players, suntanned and well dressed.

There is, psychologically, a symbiosis between Nixon and these young men. Nixon was reared in poverty and financial frustration; he grew up a physically graceless, socially awkward youth and became a man who even now finds it difficult to make small talk; he attended a small, obscure college and, as a classic "grind" in law school and in his early career, made up by perseverance and hard work what he lacked in money, social contacts, and ease of manner. His life was in marked contrast to that of these generally good-looking, easily articulate, self-confident youths. They represent the kind of young man that Richard Nixon would like to have been, thirty or thirty-five years ago.

If these young men acted out Nixon's idealized daydream of himself, they in turn took their cues from him and his senior aides. Completely orthodox in their social outlook, ferociously ambitious, intelligent but not original or erudite or intellectually curious, these young men served only their own careers. They had no guiding ethic except to do what their bosses wanted. It was no accident that two of their clichés were "at that point in time" and "in that time frame." None of them seemed to have studied any American history or political philosophy. They made occasional references to what had been done under Lyndon Johnson as if they were harking back to an ancient era.

Robert C. Odle, Jr., who had been "director of administration" —that is, office manager—of the

Hugh.W. Sloan, Jr.

Committee to Reelect the President, and Robert Reisner, who had been personal assistant to Jeb Stuart Magruder, were two of the luckier young men. They had done nothing worse than be bystanders stricken with blindness. On the day of the arrests, Magruder called Reisner from California and asked him to take home over the weekend some "sensitive" files including one marked "Gemstone," the code name for the material picked up from the wiretaps placed in the Democratic National Committee offices during the earlier break-in in May. Reisner gave the Gemstone file to Odle, who testified that he took it home and never looked at it.

Senator Montoya: Are you a very curious man, Mr. Odle?

Odle: I wasn't curious enough to read it that weekend. I was more curious to read *The Washington Post* to find out what was going on down at the committee.

Bruce A. Kehrli, a young assistant at the White House who deals with administrative housekeeping details, was another such bystander. With the Secret Service men standing by, he supervised the opening of Howard Hunt's safe and passed its contents on to John Dean and professed to know nothing.

Hugh W. Sloan, Jr., who had been treasurer of the Committee to Reelect the President, was the sole figure who knew something rotten was underway, tried to find out about it, and quit when he could not. As Maurice Stans's deputy on the money-raising and money-disbursing side of the campaign, he had protested to Stans when G. Gordon Liddy asked him for $83,000 in cash for an unspecified purpose. He was told, in effect, to mind his own business. But after the Watergate arrests, Sloan began to figure out what Liddy must have done

96

Herbert L. Porter

joined the White House staff as Herb Klein's deputy in the Office of Communications. Haldeman and Ehrlichman had installed him as deputy manager of the campaign because this smooth-talking, handsome, personable young man was one of the few persons in their inner circle who could also get along with John Mitchell.

The highlight of Magruder's testimony was his attempt to justify his perjury by citing the example of Rev. William Sloane Coffin, the chaplain of Yale, who had taught him ethics at Williams in the late 1950's. Since Coffin had been arrested in antiwar demonstrations and had counseled students to burn their draft cards rather than serve in Vietnam, Magruder argued that Coffin's example justified his own resort to illegality in behalf of his beliefs.

Coffin promptly countered with an article on the Op Ed Page of *The New York Times* in which he pointed out that he had violated the law openly while Magruder had done so secretly. He recalled telling Magruder during their days at Williams: "You're a nice guy, Jeb, but not yet a good man. You have lots of charm but little inner strength. And if you don't stand for something, you're apt to fall for anything."

This public exchange on ethics was perhaps a bit beside the point. If Magruder had been of ethnic background and had attended a more plebeian school, he would have been recognized immediately as that familiar urban type: the hustler.

Gordon C. Strachan, the young California lawyer who was recruited to the White House staff from a job in Richard Nixon's old Wall Street firm and who admitted destroying the Gemstone memoranda and other incriminating materials in Haldeman's files after the

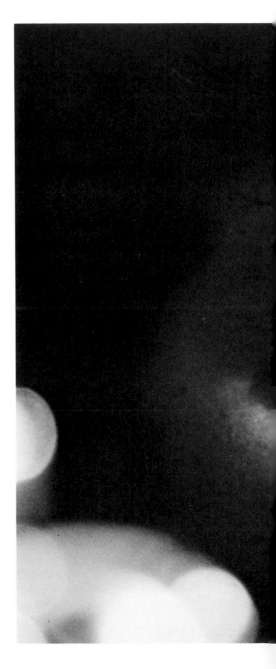

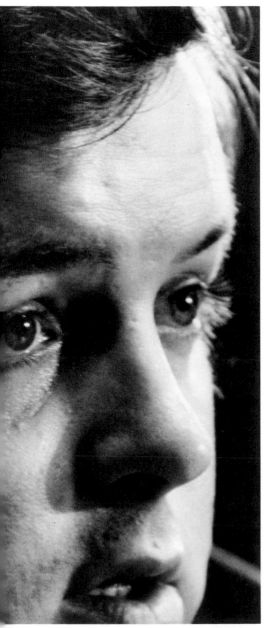

Robert Reisner

Watergate, provided the epitaph for the sad young men. Asked by Senator Montoya what advice he had to give to other young people who wanted to serve in government, Strachan said: "Stay away."

It is impossible not to feel sorry for these young men. Their hopes and in some instances their lives have been blighted. If they had served a president who by precept and example had shown them what is not done in the White House, what standards have to be observed, what sacrifices of political and personal self-interest are required by public service, they might have learned gradually and less painfully what Watergate has taught them so harshly. But who, knowing his record, would ever choose Richard Nixon as his moral preceptor?

THE ACCUSER

Few conspiracies break down unless one of the insiders decides to talk. John Dean was that insider.

Dean is an intelligent, industrious, and ambitious young man, conventional in background and orthodox in outlook. The son of a Middle Western business executive, Dean is a graduate of Staunton Military Academy, Wooster College in Ohio, and George Washington University Law School. He has the flair that truly ambitious persons have for getting to know people who can be useful and then making use of them. At Staunton, his roommate was Barry Goldwater, Jr. His first wife was Karla Hennings, the daughter of a Democratic U.S. Senator from Missouri. As a young law school graduate in Washington, Dean cultivated one of Wooster College's more influential alumni, Representative William McCulloch, then the ranking Republican on the House Judiciary Committee. Through McCulloch, he obtained a job on the Judiciary Committee staff, moved from there to a minority staff job on the National Commission for the Reform of Federal Criminal Law established during the Johnson Administration, and then contributed position papers to the Nixon campaign in 1968 that helped him get a high-ranking job in the Justice Department. He moved to the White House in 1970. At thirty-two he was counsel to the President.

What distinguished Dean from the other young staff men at the White House, the Magruders, Strachans, and Porters, was an inner toughness. On the surface, he was the ideal staff man, alert, responsive, eager to please, careful to clear decisions with higher authority. He was also willing to cooperate in the dirty work: to coach Magruder on his perjured testimony to the grand jury, to cajole and pressure General Walters to get the CIA to join the cover-up, to pass off the "hot" documents in E. Howard Hunt's safe to the hapless Pat Gray, the acting director of the FBI, with the broad hint that the latter should destroy them, and to serve as the first White House go-between in arranging the secret flow of "hush money" to keep the Watergate defendants silent.

But when McCord broke and the first cover-up began to come apart, Nixon, Haldeman, and Ehrlichman misjudged Dean, who was

hn W. Dean III

Mr. and Mrs. John Dean

shrewd enough to know he was being "set up" and tough enough to take materials from his files for a counterattack. Instead of a victim, he became the chief accuser of Richard Nixon and the White House insiders.

One of the ancient truths of politics, known to men hundreds of years before our republic was founded, is "Never strike at a king except to kill him." It took courage and careful thought under intense time pressure for Dean, an unknown young man with no private wealth or powerful friends, to decide not only to disengage from the Watergate conspiracy but also to document as best he could that the President of the United States has been the chief conspirator. Dean is not entitled to exceptional moral approbation since he was trying to save himself from prison, but he has to be credited with a daring political stroke.

His initial idea, though big, was not so daring or comprehensive. According to his testimony before the Committee, in his pivotal conversation with the President on March 21 and in subsequent talks, Dean was moving toward the conviction that Nixon's presidency could be rescued from terrible trouble only if all of those high-ranking present and former aides who were involved in Watergate—Mitchell, Haldeman, Ehrlichman, and himself, among others—acknowledged their complicity in the various crimes and conspiracies. Implicit in this joint confession was the further idea that they would agree to picture Nixon as a man who had been misled and ill-served by his senior aides and who was innocent of all but tangential or disconnected knowledge about these messy and criminal affairs. It would still be a cover-up of sorts that the public might not entirely buy, but it would be a cover-up with only one beneficiary—Nixon—and the public would be willing to accept it for the sake of allowing him to continue to function as president.

If Nixon had been willing to acknowledge the wrongs of the past, to make a clean break with that past, and to sacrifice all of the conspirators, he would have followed the turn toward honesty, the strategy of candor, that his young counsel was urging upon him in those critical days in late March. But Nixon could not reprogram himself so totally. He did not realize that so drastic a shift in personnel and in cover stories was necessary. Perhaps, too, he feared that Mitchell or some other collaborator if asked to sacrifice himself might reveal still other misdeeds of which Dean knew nothing. He replied to Dean's recounting of the whole dreadful story on March 21 with a few innocuous remarks and what seemed a baffling show of unconcern.

Reflexively, Nixon was responding with the cynical habits of a lifetime of dissembling and manipulation. He decided to hang tight with the other insiders and, with their help, to outflank Dean. Dean would be made to appear as the principal moving force in the Watergate cover-up rather than as one of several agents. It was a bold and implausible lie since Dean, despite his high-sounding title, was only a middle-level official in the White House hierarchy and had no motive to deceive his superiors and engineer a cover-up on his own. But it was no bolder or more false than previous maneuvers Nixon had successfully used against other persons as far back as Jerry Voorhis. Only over a period of several days did Dean realize that Nixon would not agree to any genuine disclosure and housecleaning, and that by attempting to force such action, he had placed himself in a lonesome and dangerous position. He set to

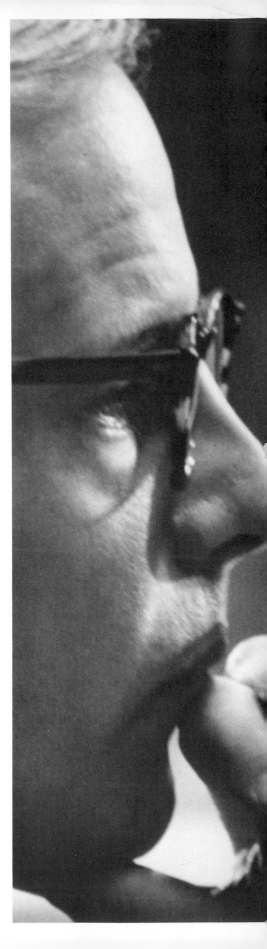

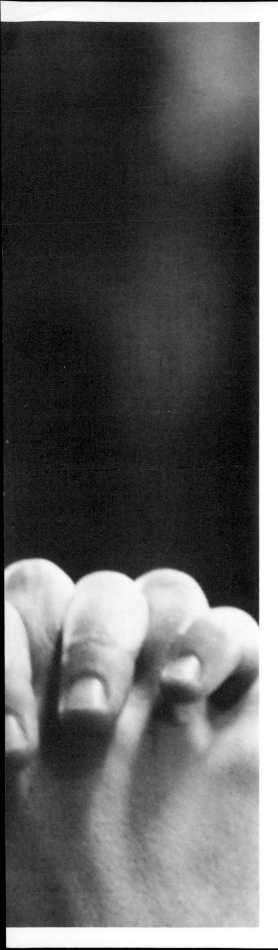

work preparing a comprehensive counterattack.

On June 25, he appeared before the Watergate Committee and in a calm monotone read a 245-page statement and submitted no fewer than forty-six supporting documents. The statement exposed not merely all he knew about the preparations for the Watergate burglaries and the subsequent cover-up, but various other misdeeds of which he had learned during three years in the White House. Dean flipped over the hard and shiny carapace of a sternly moral, law-and-order Administration and exposed the soft underbelly of crime, political repression, intrigue, and deceit.

"To one who was in the White House and became somewhat familiar with its interworkings," Dean began, "the Watergate matter was an inevitable outgrowth of a climate of excessive concern over the political impact of demonstrators, excessive concern over leaks, an insatiable appetite for political intelligence, all coupled

with a do-it-yourself White House staff, regardless of the law."

Dean recounted numerous incidents that provided the peculiar atmosphere of the Nixon White House. Two can be cited here:

I was made aware of the President's strong feelings about even the smallest of demonstrations during the late winter of 1971, when the President happened to look out the windows of the. . .White House and saw a lone man with a large ten-foot sign stretched out in front of Lafayette Park. Mr. [Lawrence] Higby [Haldeman's top aide] called me to his office to tell me of the President's displeasure with the sign in the park and told me that Mr. Haldeman said the sign had to come down. When I came out of Mr. Higby's office, I ran into Mr. Dwight Chapin [the President's appointments secretary] who said that he was going to get some "thugs" to remove that man from Lafayette Park. He said it would take him a few hours to get them, but they could do the job. I told him I didn't believe that was necessary. I then called the Secret Service and met with Mr. Louis Sims. Mr. Sims said that he felt that the Park Police could work it out. I went out with Mr. Sims, surveyed the situation, and Mr. Sims talked with the Park Police. Within thirty minutes, the man had been convinced that he should move to the back side of Lafayette Park. There the sign was out of sight from the White House. I reported back to Mr. Haldeman and after a personal look-see, he was delighted. I told Mr. Chapin he could call off the troops.

A second episode related by Dean occurred after the Pentagon Papers were published in the newspapers in June and July of 1971. Charles Colson heard that the Brookings Institution was planning the early publication of a study of Vietnam based on current documents and that Morton Halperin, a former member of Henry Kissinger's staff known to be friendly to Daniel Ellsberg, worked at Brookings.

Jack Caulfield came to me to tell me that Colson had called him in, at Ehrlichman's direction, and instructed him to burglarize the

110

Brookings Institution in an effort to determine if they had certain leaked documents. What prompted Mr. Caulfield to come to me was that he thought the matter was most unwise and that his instructions from Colson were insane. He informed me that Mr. Ulasewicz had "cased" the Brookings Institute and that . . . the security system at the Brookings building was extremely tight and it would be very difficult to break in.

Caulfield told me that he had so informed Colson, but Colson had instructed him to pursue the matter and if necessary they should plant a fire bomb in the building and retrieve the documents during the commotion that would ensue.

Convinced that Colson was intent on proceeding by one means or another, Dean flew to San Clemente and persuaded Ehrlichman that the whole operation was too risky. Ehrlichman agreed and telephoned Colson to call it off.

When testimony shows that the president's appointments secretary contemplated the hiring of thugs or that the president's special counsel recommended the firebombing of a private research institute, then a sinister figure, the political terrorist, is only one step away from the White House. It was to these desperate proposals and to similar acts of thuggery actually carried out that Senator Weicker was referring when he said to Patrick Buchanan, the White House speechwriter and ideologue, that "you people took lawlessness out of blue jeans and put it in blue suits."

Dean told the Committee of Nixon's participation in incriminating conversations concerning payments of hush money and promises of clemency to the Watergate defendants, of "orders right out of the Oval Office" directing Egil Krogh and the White House "plumbers" to burglarize the office of Ellsberg's psychiatrist, of the President's approval of the secret 1970

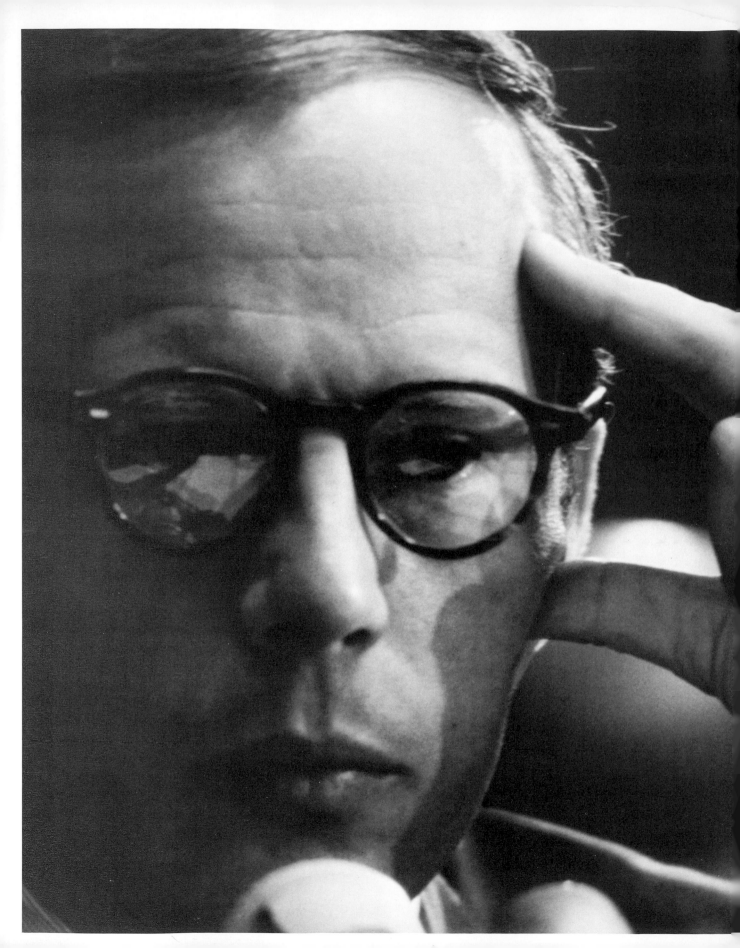

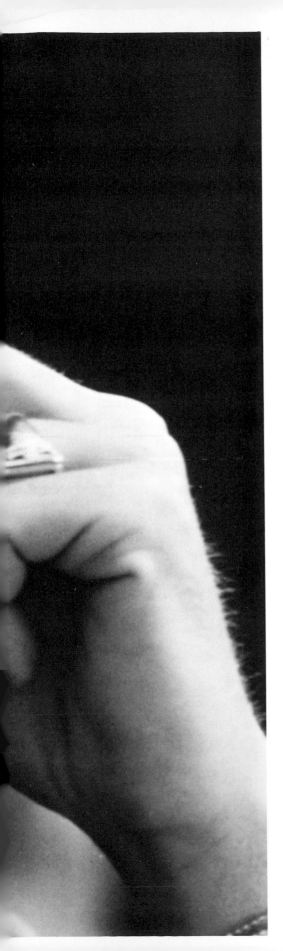

"intelligence plan" that included burglaries, illegal wiretapping, and other criminal acts, of the compiling of "enemy lists," and of the President's resolute determination to use the Internal Revenue Service and other federal agencies to harass, intimidate, and, if possible, ruin his political opponents and his critics in the press.

Dean sat through four full days of cross-examination but, except for trivial confusion in the names of two Washington hotels, he was not shaken on a single factual statement. When his testimony was concluded, *The Wall Street Journal* editorialized: "Mr. Dean's account is quite enough for a prima facie case, to create the presumption of presidential involvement, to shift the burden of proof to the White House."

Columnist Stewart Alsop, another commentator friendly to the President, wrote in *Newsweek:* "To continue to believe that President Nixon was wholly innocent of any involvement in the Watergate cover-up requires, by this time, a major act of faith. . . . If the pro-Nixon witnesses, or Mr. Nixon himself, can extricate the President from the web John Dean has woven, it will be a miracle."

No miracle was to occur. If John Dean had not politically killed the king he once served, he had shaken that ruler's house to its foundations and stripped him of all moral authority.

POLS AND BAGMEN

John Mitchell is an object lesson in the costs of enlisting in Richard Nixon's service. In late 1967, when he began to be active in Nixon's drive for the Republican presidential nomination, John Mitchell was known for two things: he was an expert in the arcane subject of laws affecting the issuance of municipal bonds, and he was the man who had merged his stodgy but profitable law practice with that of Richard Nixon. Two campaigns and six years later, Mitchell's family life was in ruins and his law practice null; he was estranged from the President and faced multiple indictments on numerous criminal charges.

By July 10, when he followed his one-time protégé John Dean to the witness chair, Mitchell and former Secretary of Commerce Maurice Stans were already under indictment for allegedly using their influence with the Securities and Exchange Commission on behalf of financier Robert Vesco in exchange for a cash contribution of $200,000 to the Nixon campaign. Mitchell also faced renewed investigation by Special Prosecutor Archibald Cox for his part in settling an antitrust suit against International Telephone and Telegraph on favorable terms. ITT at the time was offering $400,000 to defray the costs of the 1972 Republican National Convention. ITT lobbyist Dita Beard had written in her notorious memorandum: "Mitchell is definitely helping us, but it cannot be known."

The Watergate charges were thus the third in a series of staggering legal difficulties that beset Mitchell. Before his appearance, there had been rumors that he had been drinking heavily and was perhaps on the verge of a nervous crack-up. Mitchell's demeanor belied those rumors. He kept unshakably to his own curious version of events, a version halfway between the revelations of Dean and Magruder and the buttoned-up, concede-'em-nothing scenario offered later by Ehrlichman and Haldeman.

Mitchell denied that he had approved Liddy's plan to wiretap the Democrats or that he had seen the "Gemstone" memoranda summarizing those taps. Magruder's testimony to that effect was "a

115

hn N. Mitchell

palpable, damnable lie."

But Mitchell conceded that he had participated in much, though not all, of the cover-up. In his version of events, he was not concerned that the truth about the burglary would come out. His worries were the earlier break-in of Ellsberg's psychiatrist and other misdeeds that he characterized as "the White House horrors." If known, they would have seriously damaged Nixon's campaign.

"In my mind," Mitchell said, responding to a question from Senator Talmadge, "the reelection of Richard Nixon compared with what was available on the other side was so much more important that I put it in just that context."

Throughout his three days in the witness chair, Mitchell studded his testimony with the language of pseudo-tough masculinity. When Committee Counsel Sam Dash asked him why he had not thrown Liddy out of his office the very first time he proposed his "intelligence plan," Mitchell replied: "I should have thrown him out of the window."

Discussing the cover-up he arranged for the Watergate participants, Mitchell said: "It would have been simpler to have shot them all."

During John Dean's testimony, Senator Inouye had asked him a series of questions prepared by White House Counsel Fred Buzhardt, strongly suggesting that the cover-up was wholly the work of Dean and Mitchell. The following day, the White House disavowed the questions: Nixon apparently did not wish to risk a rift with Mitchell in advance of his appearance before the Committee. Despite this clear evidence that his former chief might be prepared to disown him, Mitchell asserted Nixon's innocence. In none of those telephone conversations or those quiet cruises down the Potomac on the White House yacht on summer evenings had the President ever asked him a question about Watergate. Had Nixon done so, Mitchell said, "I would have spelled it out chapter and verse.

Unlike Dean, Mitchell felt he might be safer in the long run if he did not break away from such shelter as the White House still afforded him. It was the last thin hope of one who had enlisted in Richard Nixon's entourage, ridden to power, done his share of dirty work, and been sure he could survive. He had mistaken himself for an old political pro. He now found he was very much alone.

Richard A. Moore, a Yale-educated lawyer who became wealthy managing the radio and television interests of *The Los Angeles Times,* serves as one of Nixon's public relations advisers with the title of special counsel. Since Dean had partially confided in him during the weeks of transition in March and April when he was breaking with the White House, the Committee called Moore to hear his version.

"I serve primarily as an extra hand—as a source of white-haired advice—whenever the President or the younger men with line responsibility ask my help," Moore explained.

Moore was painfully eager to affirm his loyalty to the President and his faith in the President's innocence, but his testimony provided only a muddled interlude. Subjected to an aggressive examination by Assistant Counsel Terry Lenzner, Moore appeared badly shaken, remarking at one point, "I'll let the answer stand, whatever it is."

The next day he lamely observed: "I certainly wish that the minute I began to get suspicious, I had gone to the President."

With Herbert W. Kalmbach, the Committee was back in the middle of the Nixon operation. Through his long-term friendship with Robert Finch, Nixon's protégé and first Secretary of Health, Education and Welfare, Kalmbach entered the Nixon inner circle. He became Nixon's personal attorney, arranged the purchase of the San Clemente estate, and prepared Nixon's income tax returns. Having raised more than $6,000,000 in the 1968 campaign, Kalmbach was put in charge of that campaign's secret surplus of $2,470,000. It became, in effect, a revolving slush fund that paid the salary of Tony Ulasewicz and later of "dirty tricks" operative Donald Segretti, that financed much of the campaign against George C. Wallace in the Alabama gubernatorial race in 1970, and that paid for other secret Nixon political projects. Kalmbach's known access to the President boomed his law firm:

United Air Lines, the Music Corporation of America, Travelers Insurance, Atlantic-Richfield, and other national corporations suddenly decided after 1968 that they needed Kalmbach's legal advice.

Kalmbach raised the money for the Nixon reelection campaign until Maurice Stans quit as Secretary of Commerce to take charge. In the summer of 1972, it was to Kalmbach that Dean turned to obtain money for the Watergate defendants.

Preceded by his menacing reputation as one of the President's principal bagmen, Kalmbach proved to be a dignified and rather appealing witness. With a long, big-featured face, the sad eyes of a basset hound, and a grave voice, Kalmbach was like a spy who had come in from the cold after a hard, even harrowing, tour of duty. The Committee's questioning elicited probably about one-tenth of what he knows of Nixon's activities, but what he told corroborated Dean's account of the early financing of the cover-up.

The only animus that showed through in Kalmbach's restrained testimony was his feeling of betrayal by John Ehrlichman, whom he had thought a friend and a trusted collaborator.

". . . Well, I can't describe to you, Senator," he said to Weicker, "the feeling that I had when I learned that I had been taped [by Ehrlichman]. It was just as if I had been kicked in the stomach."

Kalmbach described the interview he sought with Ehrlichman in the summer of 1972 to seek reassurance about his money-raising for the Watergate defendants.

I can remember it very vividly because I looked at him, and I said, John, I am looking right into your eyes. I know Jeanne and

118

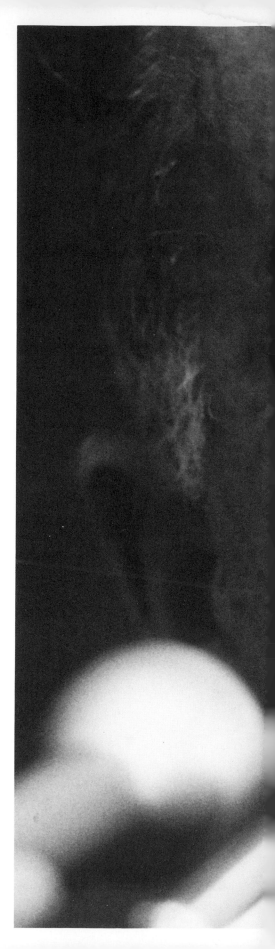

your family, you know Barbara and my family. I said, you know that my family and my reputation mean everything to me, and it is just absolutely necessary, John, that you tell me, first, that John Dean has the authority to direct me in this assignment, that it is a proper assignment and that I am to go forward on it.

Dash: And did he look you in the eyes?

Kalmbach: Yes he did.

Dash: What did he say to you?

Kalmbach: He said, Herb, John Dean does have the authority. It is proper, and you are to go forward.

Tony Ulasewicz, the paunchy, jowly retired detective who served as Kalmbach's agent in the delivery of the money to the Watergate burglars, provided the hearings with their only sustained comic relief. With vivid colloquialisms, deadpan delivery, and the street-wise attitudes of an old cop who has spent his professional life on intimate terms with sin, Ulasewicz seemed to have stepped into the Caucus Room out of the pages of Damon Runyon.

Hunt had sent Dean this message: "The writer has a manuscript of a play to sell." Kalmbach invited Ulasewicz to his hotel room in Washington and gave him $75,000 in $100 bills to "buy the manuscript." Since Ulasewicz had no briefcase, he stuffed the money into a hotel laundry bag, subsequently referring to the bribes he transported as "the laundry." Kalmbach's instructions were to transfer the money to Hunt through one of the several lawyers in the case. But the first two he approached "showed no interest in any script, players, or any type of message that I would give," Ulasewicz testified. "Running around with $75,000, trying to get rid of it, was becoming a problem."

121

Anthony T. Ulasewicz

Since he could make no move without first checking it with Kalmbach, he had to make so many calls that he began wearing a bus conductor's change dispenser around his waist to carry all the dimes he needed. "I began to call them Kalmbach comeback calls," he testified.

He finally made contact with Hunt's attorney, William O. Bittman, who proved willing to take $25,000 in cash. Ulasewicz left the money for him in an envelope on the rack of telephone directories in the lobby of Bittman's office building.

Then began his contacts with Mrs. Hunt, later to be killed in a Chicago plane accident, and invariably referred to as "the writer's wife." He made his deliveries of cash to her at the National Airport. "I would go into this telephone booth and underneath where the coin drop is, I would Scotch tape the key to the locker where I made my drop."

Mrs. Hunt would arrive at the appointed time, retrieve the locker key from its hiding place in the public telephone booth, open the locker, take the packet of money, and leave. But her demands for money steadily escalated. By mid-September, according to Ulasewicz's testimony, these demands totaled more than $400,000. When Ulasewicz flew to California to pick up another block of cash, Kalmbach said, "Tony, what's your opinion of all this?"

I said, "Well, Mr. Kalmbach, I will tell you, something here is not kosher. It's definitely not your ball game, Mr. Kalmbach. Whatever has happened, we started with no negotiations, we are into negotiations; we started with $75,000, and we have now got something like $220,000 coming in and we are only approaching half. I know that the next conversation I have that figure has got to go up, from all the inferences and all."

Kalmbach agreed it was not his ball game. He

122

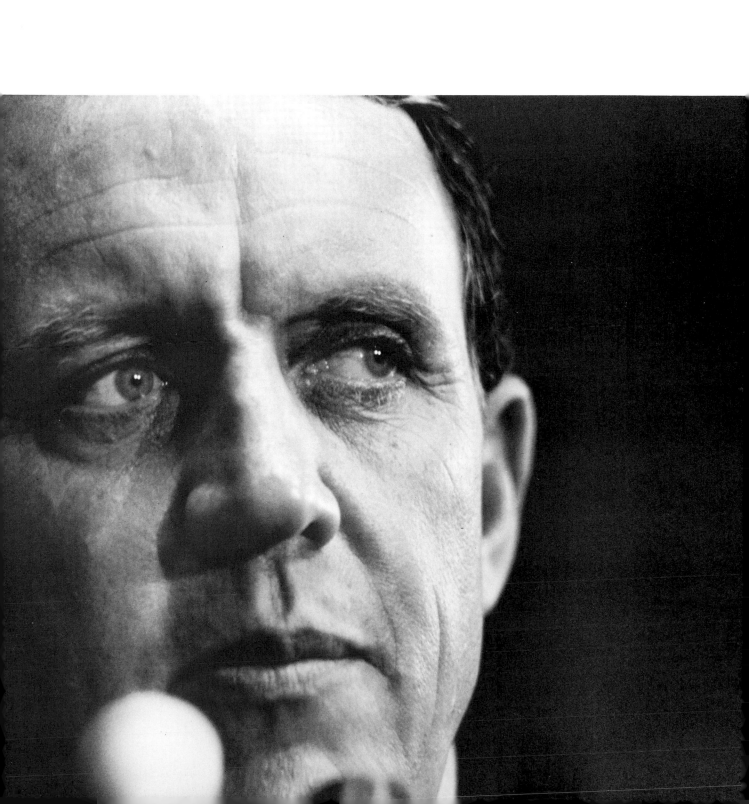

and the amiable Tony dropped out of the money-passing game in late September 1972.

Kalmbach's successor was mysterious, close-mouthed Frederick C. LaRue, an alumnus of the Goldwater movement. LaRue is as responsible as any single man for putting Nixon in the White House. He was G.O.P. national committeeman from Mississippi, where his father, originally a Texan, had struck it rich in oil. He did not meet Nixon until 1965, but they soon formed an alliance. They agreed that the Goldwaterites could come to power in 1968 under Nixon's leadership, but only if they stayed in the background and permitted him to present a moderate image. Working in tandem with Senator Strom Thurmond of South Carolina, LaRue kept in line the rank-and-file Southern delegates who wanted to bolt to Ronald Reagan. He thereby saved Nixon's Southern base at the 1968 convention.

After the election, LaRue had a desk in the White House and worked without pay as a political undercover man, mostly in the South. In early 1973 a news story reported—accurately, as it turned out—that immediately after the Watergate burglary, LaRue had supervised a purge of all incriminating records at the Committee to Reelect. A former White House colleague was asked if this was true. "I don't know," he replied, "but I do know that if it had been up to Fred LaRue, there wouldn't have been any records to destroy in the first place."

Gordon Strachan testified about going to LaRue's apartment in the Watergate to deliver $280,000 in cash that had been in Haldeman's safekeeping at the White House and that was to be used for further payments to the Watergate defendants and their lawyers. Before

Frederick C. LaRue

taking the money, LaRue put on a pair of gloves and said, "I never saw you."

LaRue pleaded guilty to one count of obstructing justice and cooperated with Special Prosecutor Cox, but his appearance before the Watergate Committee was anticlimactic and unrevealing. Hollow-cheeked, thin-lipped, and modishly bespectacled, he was Flem Snopes brought to judgment, defeated for now but sure to come boring back when opportunity presented itself. His only memorable line was yet another example of Mitchell's tough-guy prose. LaRue testified that when Magruder, shortly after the June 17 arrests, discussed the incriminating Gemstone file, Mitchell said: "It might be a good idea if Mr. Magruder had a fire."

Robert C. Mardian, who followed LaRue to the witness chair, is another little-known, deeply reactionary member of the Goldwater faction. The son of a wealthy Armenian immigrant, Mardian had practiced law in Southern California. He, along with Richard Kleindienst, William Rehnquist, and others from the Goldwater group, effectively ran most of the Justice Department during Mitchell's tenure. As Assistant Attorney General for Internal Security, Mardian initiated numerous cases against antiwar protesters and radical dissenters, virtually all of them ultimately unsuccessful. He was disappointed not to have been promoted to higher office in the Justice Department and then again not to have been named deputy director of the Committee to Reelect the President, a post that went to the much younger and—from the Haldeman-Ehrlichman standpoint—more obedient and pliable Magruder. Mardian was fobbed off with the job of "political coordinator." But after the June 17 arrests, Mitchell turned to him and to LaRue to clean out the files,

126

Robert C. Mardian

128

Maurice H. Stans

keep tight control over the staff, and help coordinate the cover-up. During the summer and fall of 1972, Mardian was the "house lawyer" at the Committee office at 1701 Pennsylvania Avenue, just as Dean was "house lawyer" at 1600 Pennsylvania Avenue. His involvement in the illegality and deceit of this fiasco was the final bitter draught for Mardian, a proud, ambitious man who is somber by nature and a conservative ideologue by conviction. His statement to the Committee expressed something of his rage and disappointment:

. . . The information that I received on the morning of June 17 and June 21 [from Liddy and Magruder] was the most shocking experience in my entire legal career. The facts thus learned thrust me into a situation which I can only compare, in terms of personal anxiety, to being caught in quicksand. Information was imparted to me bit by bit, much of it contradictory, which drew me inexorably into an intolerable and, at times, unbearable situation of personal conscience. A situation in which I was precluded from acting according to the dictates of my personal desires or interests; a situation in which ultimately my only hope was the selfish one of not becoming implicated in the conduct of others who I felt it my duty to serve.

To those who cherish it, money can bring a sense of invulnerability and provide its own absolution. Maurice Stans is one of money's true believers. Starting in poverty, he mastered the arts of accountancy and was executive partner of his firm at thirty-two. In a long business career he amassed millions assiduously and sometimes ruthlessly. In public life, as Deputy Postmaster General and Budget Director in the Eisenhower Administration and Secretary of Commerce in the Nixon Administration, he cultivated the reputation of a nickel-nurser of public funds. In politics, as fund-raiser in successive Nixon campaigns, he set records for his skill and persistence in shaking every money tree.

Stans, a slim, handsome, graying sixty-five, his hooded eyes rimmed with tiny wrinkles, his voice light and calm, was an impenetrable witness. He might have been attending a not very interesting board meeting. Except for an occasional arching of the eyebrows or a thin smile, his face was expressionless. Well tailored as always during his three days of testimony, he wore on different days a tiny American flag in his lapel, and cufflinks and a tieclasp bearing the presidential seal, all gifts from Nixon. Most of all, he was clothed in the imperturbability of money.

After his lawyer had made a pro forma objection to his being called as a witness because he was already under indictment with Mitchell for perjury in the Vesco Case in New York, Stans professed his willingness to cooperate with the committee. But throughout, he disclaimed personal knowledge of every disputed event and conceded nothing. Hugh Sloan, his young treasurer, had earlier testified of his worry about the first cash payment of $83,000 to Liddy for an undisclosed purpose and had quoted Stans's significant rejoinder after a conference with Mitchell: "I do not want to know and you do not want to know." Stans blandly put this remark "in context," explaining that he had experienced total frustration in dealing with the operational side of the campaign headed by Mitchell and Magruder:

The remark I made, and I cannot quote it precisely, was something to the effect that "I don't know what's going on in this campaign and I don't think you ought to try to know." We were the cashiers, we received the money, and we paid the bills. They had responsibility for everything they did. It did not seem that it was incumbent upon us to question the propriety of any payment, whether it was to Mr. Liddy or anybody else, and we did not.

Under heavy questioning, Stans held to this image of himself as the innocent cashier. Although the

committee had already learned from Magruder that
he and Mitchell had acquainted Stans with some of the
facts of the Watergate operation on June 24, one week after
the arrests, Stans testified that he could remember no
such meeting and learned nothing about Watergate until
the public disclosures nine months later in March 1973.
Although Liddy had been legal counsel to Stans's Finance
Committee until he was fired after the burglary and
although Sloan had resigned as treasurer because of the
pressure on him to commit perjury, Stans said he had
inquired into neither of these developments.

    Regarding the strictly financial side of the
campaign, Stans was again unforthcoming. He had no idea
how Barker, the head of the Watergate burglars, came to
have $114,000 of the committee's funds in his bank
account. He had destroyed records of campaign
contributions only to protect the privacy of contributors.
He gave Kalmbach $75,000 in cash for the first payment
to the Watergate defendants but never asked him what
he wanted the money for.

    No witness, not even John Ehrlichman at his
most aggressive, irked the members of the committee as
much as Stans. It was apparent they did not feel that he was
"leveling" with them, but they could not get through
that smooth exterior. Senator Ervin took out after him
aggressively on the subject of the destroyed financial
records.

Q. Why are there not complete records in existence?
A. Well, at one time, Mr. Chairman, some of the records were
    removed from the committee's files and destroyed.
Q. Why were they destroyed?
A. They were destroyed because there was no requirement that
    they be kept, and insofar as contributors were concerned we
    wanted to respect the anonymity that they had sought and

that they were then entitled to under the law. We are talking now about contributions before April 17, 1972,

Q. Were they destroyed before or after the break-in?

A. They were destroyed after the break-in and I would insist, Mr. Chairman, that there is no relevance between the two.

Q. You swear, you are stating upon your oath that there is no connection between the destruction of these records and the break-in of the Watergate or any fear that the press or the public might find out from these records what the truth was about these matters?

A. Well, let me speak only with respect to myself. I will say to you that there was no connection between my destruction of the summary sheets given to me by Mr. Sloan and the Watergate affair.

Q. Well, it was quite a queer coincidence, was it not?

A. It would . . .

Q. Rather a suspicious coincidence that the records which showed these matters were destroyed six days after the break-in at the Watergate?

A. Mr. Chairman, the adjectives are yours.

Q. Sir?

A. The adjectives that you are using, *queer, coincidence,* and *suspicion.*

Q. Don't you think it is rather suspicious?

A. No, I do not think so, Senator.

Q. Do you think it is kind of normal to expect people who had records concerning outlays of campaign funds to destroy those records after five men were caught in an act of burglary with money from the committee in their pockets?

A. [It] was pure and innocent coincidence.

Senator Talmadge tried one of his shrewd forays. He got Stans to agree that his previous testimony had been that he devoted his whole time to raising money and did not get into "small detailed things." Then he read a Stans memorandum: "It will be necessary for us to establish a system of control over the purchasing and distribution of all articles, such as bumper strips, banners, pins, jewelry and so forth."

132

Did not that indicate that Stans had interested himself in many details of the Nixon campaign?

Stans countered that detailed accounting of articles like jewelry and pins was required under the new campaign law. Talmadge then showed that this could not be the reason because the new law did not go into effect until April 7 and this memorandum was dated February 28, 1972.

Talmadge called attention to disbursements in cash totaling $1,777,000 to various persons who spent the money for espionage, sabotage, suborning perjury, and other activities that turned out to be either illegal or highly questionable. Stans had disclaimed any knowledge of how that money was spent.

"You are considered to be one of the most able certified public accountants in America. Why did you worry about bumper strips instead of those funds?" Talmadge asked.

It was an unanswerable question and dominated the next day's news stories. But it did not shake Stans. He bade farewell to the committee with a statement defending the "innocent victims of this tragedy. I put myself in that category. . . . When you write your report, you give me back my good name."

Richard A. Moore

133

John D. Erlichman

MR. OUTSIDE

They had been known in their days of White House power as "the Germans," "the Berlin Wall," or as "Mr. Outside and Mr. Inside." John D. Ehrlichman, the former zoning lawyer from Seattle who had a gift for small talk and made himself available occasionally to members of the press and of Congress, was regarded as the more affable "Mr. Outside." H. R. Haldeman, his UCLA classmate who came to the top staff job in the White House from a career in the J. Walter Thompson advertising firm, once said, "Every president needs an S.O.B. I'm Nixon's." Tireless in his attention to detail, tyrannical to his subordinates, implacable in his acquisition of power, Haldeman was the inaccessible "Mr. Inside."

In their successive appearances before the Committee, however, they reversed their public images: Ehrlichman coming on like gangbusters, hostile and combative; Haldeman, all soft deference and prep school manners. However, beneath their dissimilar styles, they shared a common alliance with Nixon, a common arrogance, and a common lawyer. John J. Wilson, their irascible, aggressive attorney, is diminutive (five feet four inches), old (he celebrated his seventy-second birthday during Ehrlichman's appearance), deeply conservative, and exceptionally able.

For most of a day, Wilson had the press and the Committee chasing a legal hare into a dense constitutional thicket. Exploiting Senator Ervin's patent desire to run a fair hearing, Wilson took time to argue that Nixon had the inherent power to order the burglary of Dr. Fielding's office to protect the nation against foreign spies. Factually, it was an odd argument since Nixon denied that he had ordered the Fielding burglary, Ehrlichman denied any

137

prior knowledge of it, and the FBI found no evidence
to link Daniel Ellsberg with any foreign power.

Administration supporters had hoped that
Wilson would be their grand old man to offset Senator
Ervin. However, while Haldeman was testifying directly
after Ehrlichman, Wilson ruined that public relations
dream when he casually referred to Senator Inouye during
a recess exchange with reporters as "the little Jap."

From the outset, Ehrlichman took the offensive.

"I didn't cover up anything to do with
Watergate," he declared flatly in his opening statement.

He depicted himself and Nixon as too busy with
high public policy to think about mere politics. "The
vast percentage of my working time was spent on
substantive issues and domestic policy. About one half of
one percent was spent on politics, the campaign, and the
events with which you have been concerning yourself
as a committee," he said.

Soon after Sam Dash began his initial
interrogation, Ehrlichman flashed one of his terrifying,
downward-curving smiles and scornfully interjected,
"Now I am arguing with the professor . . ."

When Ervin delivered a homily about the
Fourth Amendment, Ehrlichman briskly commented:
"I think the thing that your argument artfully chooses
to avoid dealing with . . ."

"I'm not trying to avoid anything," Ervin said.

"Now you've interrupted me," Ehrlichman
pressed on. "You have a delightful trial-room practice of
interrupting something you don't want to hear."

To Senator Weicker, he aggressively defended
the hiring of Tony Ulasewicz to dig up "dirt" about the
drinking, sex lives, and personal habits of Administration

139

John J. Wilson

opponents. When Weicker incredulously asked whether
he thought that kind of material had any place in political
debate, Ehrlichman asserted that it did.

Ehrlichman did not hesitate to take on the
politically sacrosanct dead such as J. Edgar Hoover. He
described a memo from Hoover as "window dressing . . .
old-hat stuff . . . stale bread."

"I don't think it's possible to make a case that
the bureau was just on its tippytoes doing everything it
should," he said.

Less striking but more significant were his
denials. He had "no recollection" of requesting the CIA to
assist Howard Hunt. He denied prior knowledge or
approval of the plan to burglarize Dr. Fielding's office
although he acknowledged endorsing a "covert" mission
to obtain Ellsberg's psychiatric files as long as it could
not be traced to the White House. "There are a lot of
perfectly legal ways that medical information is leaked,"
he asserted.

He denied knowing anything about Kalmbach's

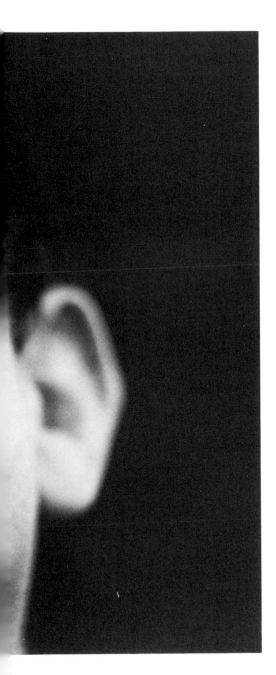

role in raising money for the defendants. He ridiculed Kalmbach's account of their interview. "I am sure that if . . . I had looked into his eyes and we had invoked the names of our wives . . . I would remember that solemn occasion," he said, baring his teeth in another of his terrifying smiles.

He said he had never asked Gray to destroy the documents from Hunt's safe, had never discussed clemency for the Watergate defendants, and had no inkling that a cover-up was underway. In short, the Nixon-Haldeman-Ehrlichman line would be one of total denial of any wrongdoing or impropriety. Ehrlichman's words foreshadowed Haldeman's testimony and Nixon's opaque and unrepentant answers at his August news conference.

If everything Ehrlichman said were true, it was impossible to understand why he had been forced to resign from office or why he was even being questioned by the committee. By his own account, he had been a paragon of duty, discretion, and integrity. Yet on significant points, his testimony was contradicted by that of Mitchell, Dean, Kalmbach, Sloan, Gray, and former CIA Director Richard Helms.

Moreover, despite Ehrlichman's volubility and aggressive, blustering tone, his testimony was often curiously vague. Pressed to relate what had taken place during meetings lasting an hour or two hours or more in the President's office, he would reiterate: "We discussed how to get this whole story out." Or, "We discussed executive privilege."

He also had evasive phrases which he made use of with increasing frequency: "I am not your best witness on that. . . . This was not my beat. . . . I didn't have a feel for that. . . . I had to get up to speed on this."

The Senators did not conceal their disbelief. Senator Inouye, thinking his microphone was dead, exclaimed: "What a liar!"

On another day, Senator Talmadge said: "I do not believe all this could take place in the White House without you knowing about it. Do you mean to tell me that you, as one of the highest officials in the land, sat there in the White House after authorizing the sum of $350,000 to pay for lawyers' fees, bail bond, and everything else in the cover-up, supremely ignorant that you were obstructing justice?"

Long after most people had forgotten the wrangling over who knew what and who had said what to whom, they would remember two chilling remarks from Ehrlichman. Of L. Patrick Gray III in his losing battle for confirmation as FBI Director, Ehrlichman acknowledged with a smile that he had said: "Let him hang there. . . . Let him twist slowly, slowly in the wind."

Explaining why, after he ceased to be White House counsel, he had lost touch with Tony Ulasewicz's work, he said, again with a smile, "Ulasewicz was a facility that went with the job."

If he thought of Gray as a corpse and Ulasewicz as a facility, what did John Ehrlichman think of himself?

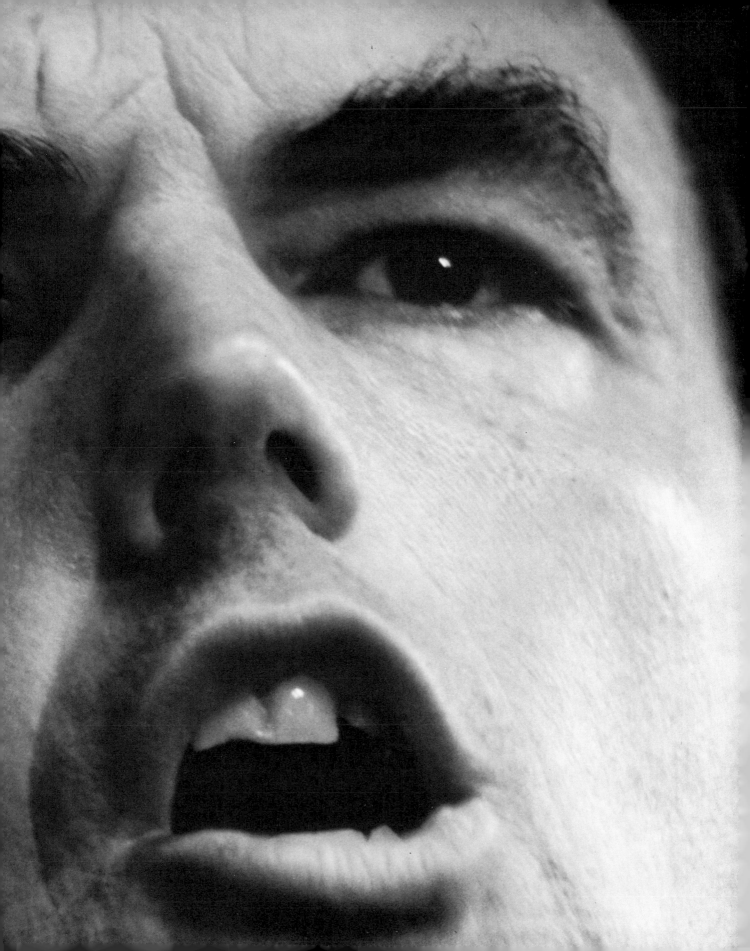

MR. INSIDE

Harry Robbins Haldeman had practiced two professions before entering the White House in 1969. In business, he had been an advertising man. In politics, he had been an advance man. Advertising men are paid to worry less about the substance of a client's product than about its image in the marketplace. Advance men are hired to worry not about what the candidate says but about the physical circumstances in which he says it: the length of the parade route, the size of the hall, the arrangements for the VIP reception.

As an advertising man, Haldeman supervised the accounts of Seven-Up, Sani-Flush, Griffin shoe polish, and Black Flag insecticide. He was not a stylish copywriter or a hard-drinking salesman; he was a meticulous administrator. In twenty years with the J. Walter Thompson advertising agency, he rose to become head of its Los Angeles office because he was good at manipulating images, at keeping the sales pitch simple and uncluttered, at telling the customer no more than he needed to know to remember the product. As an advance man, Haldeman never lost track of a detail: he knew how many cars had to be rented and how many hotel rooms reserved; he knew when the motorcade would pass a certain corner and when the balloons should be released; he knew how many people had to be bussed in for the "spontaneous" demonstration and how many "home-made, hand-lettered" signs they would need. Haldeman was an advance man in Nixon's vice-presidential campaign in 1956, chief advance man in 1960, and campaign manager in the losing gubernatorial campaign in 1962.

He and his candidate were deeply compatible. If Nixon's campaigns were intellectually empty, they were smoothly run, strong on selling a few basic images, and not averse to a little deceptive "market research." Thus, in the 1962 campaign, Haldeman set up a dummy organization known as the Committee for the Preservation of the Democratic Party in California. It sent to 900,000 Democratic voters a mailing that purported to be a poll. The recipients were asked to answer questions such as whether they agreed that Nixon's opponent was an "extremist" and whether they would be willing to contribute money to

149

the committee in its fight to get the Democratic Party back on the track. Two years after that campaign, a Superior Court judge in California ruled that this mail poll was a fraud, that "Mr. Nixon and Mr. Haldeman approved the plan and project," and that the funds had been "solicited for the use, benefit and furtherance of Richard M. Nixon."

In his four years in the White House as Nixon's chief of staff, Haldeman kept the habits and preoccupations of his two professions. He did not inject himself in disputes over policy. But once Nixon laid down what the policy was to be, Haldeman enforced strict obedience. He kept track of every visitor and every piece of paper going to the President's office, and he gradually came to control every subordinate appointment in the White House, no matter how lowly. He installed young Ron Ziegler, one of his account executives, as press secretary, and monitored every press release and news conference answer Ziegler put out. When the Committee to Reelect the President was set up, he installed Jeb Stuart Magruder as deputy manager to be a check on John Mitchell's power as manager. He assigned Gordon Strachan as his personal agent at the Committee to attend all meetings and receive copies of every piece of paper. No advertising or promotional materials could be used without Haldeman's personal approval. Travel schedules not only for Nixon but for all of his surrogate campaigners had to be cleared with Haldeman.

As a witness before the Senate Watergate Committee, Haldeman used the talents of the advertising man in the service of the advance man. He had a simple message to sell: everything was John Dean's fault. "As it now appears, we were badly misled by one or more of the principals and even more so by our own man

[Dean], for reasons which are still not completely clear."

He told the Committee and the customers in the television audience nothing that did not square neatly with Ehrlichman's basic testimony. Once again, the picture was painted of himself, Ehrlichman, and the President as a trio of busy innocents: "The President raised questions as to the facts of Watergate from time to time during the period of June through the election. His interest consistently was to get the facts and get them out."

The old advance man who until recently had been deciding such details as who on the White House staff could have a reserved parking space or eat in the White House mess now told the Committee that he hardly paid any attention to much that was going on around him and could remember almost nothing.

Had Dean asked his approval to request Kalmbach to raise funds for the Watergate defendants? "I do not recall such a request."

Was he aware of how Kalmbach had handled the surplus funds from the 1968 campaign? "I am not familiar with all the specifics of sources, amounts, or disbursements of these funds, although Mr. Kalmbach did keep me periodically posted on his activities in this area."

Since he had told Dean to take the $350,000 under his [Haldeman's] control and give it to the Watergate defendants, did he not have some concern or sense of responsibility for how the money was used? "My involvement in the transfer of funds was entirely through John Dean. . . . Since John Dean never stated at the time that the funds would be used for any other than legal and proper purposes, I had no reason to question the propriety or legality of the process of delivering

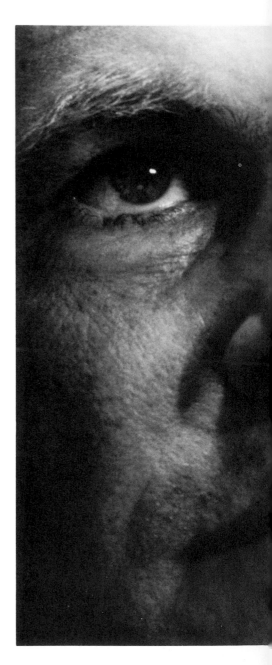

152

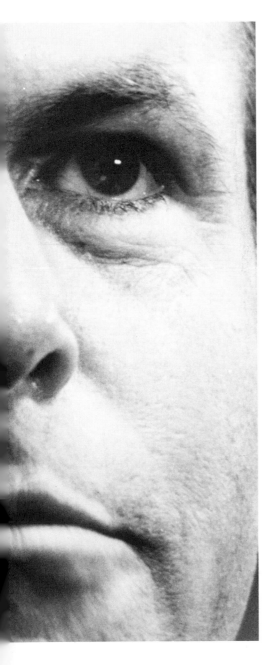

the $350,000 to the Committee via LaRue.

What about the "intelligence reports" code-named "Sedan Chair" and "Gemstone" that Strachan transmitted to him from the Committee to Reelect? "I have absolutely no recollection of seeing any such report and it is quite likely that I did not see it even if it was included in a Strachan transmission to me, since I rarely, if ever, read through or even looked at all of the materials that he sent in to me in these reports."

What of Strachan's testimony that Haldeman had told him to "make sure the files are clean"? "I have no recollection of giving Mr. Strachan instructions to destroy any materials."

What about the memorandum to him from Charles Colson on March 30, 1972, warning that Mitchell and other Administration witnesses might have committed perjury before the Senate Judiciary Committee concerning their dealings with ITT? Haldeman said he was "not familiar" with the memorandum. After reading it, he still had "no recollection" of it.

Why in 1971 had he ordered an investigation by the FBI of Columbia Broadcasting newsman Daniel Schorr? Was it, as Schorr believed, to try to find damaging material? Or was it, as Ron Ziegler had said at the time, that Schorr was under consideration for an Administration appointment? Haldeman conceded that Ziegler's explanation was false, but said, "I simply don't recall what the reason was for it."

Had he requested twenty-four-hour surveillance of Senator Edward Kennedy?

"I am not familiar with the specifics of the reason for the request."

153

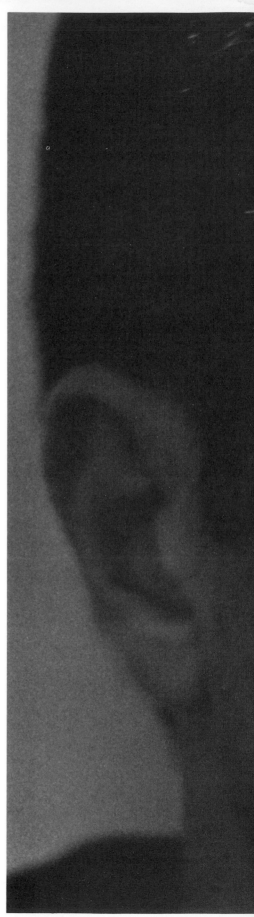

When had he first learned of the Watergate break-in?

"That seems to be the crucial question, and I have to give, I guess, the most incredible answer. I don't know, Mr. Dash. I simply don't remember how I learned about it or precisely when or from whom."

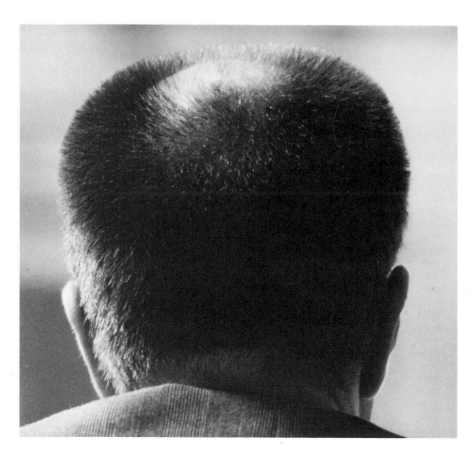

Richard M. Helms

THE OLD BUREAUCRATS

They were a battered company, these eight veterans of the national security establishment. Each of them had been used by Richard Nixon and his adjutants, a few grievously used. Each knew something about the inner politics of the bureaucracies, and had tried to protect himself or his agency or both when he was caught up in the secret games of the White House players. None had wholly succeeded, none had walked away with both his power and his reputation intact. Some were now politically dead and some among the walking wounded.

Richard M. Helms, tall, slim, aristocratic-looking, had come out of the best schools—he spent two high school years in Switzerland and Germany and graduated from Williams College—and wartime service in the Office of Strategic Services to spend a lifetime in the Central Intelligence Agency, acting as its chief from 1966 to 1973. Throughout the Nixon Administration, Helms fought a losing battle for influence. He and the President were never on the same personal wavelength. On issues of military intelligence, the President leaned toward the rival estimates prepared by the Pentagon. On political and diplomatic trends, the CIA's work did not always meet with Henry Kissinger's approval. A fear grew in the agency that the intelligence service was headed for the same wasteland as the State Department's Foreign Service. Helms, low-keyed, shrewd, hard-working, strove to please the White House, to fend off his rivals in military intelligence, and to sustain the morale of his subordinates. Early in 1973, he was finally shunted aside and sent into virtual exile as Ambassador to Iran.

Though a nonpolitical career man, Helms was distrusted as a holdover from the previous Administration. Nixon followed the technique of appointing deputy directors of CIA who were personally loyal to himself. The first was General Robert Cushman, who had been his military aide. When Cushman departed to head the Marine Corps, Nixon chose General Vernon Walters, an Army linguist who had been his interpreter. It was to these deputies that the White House turned for help on their special projects. In 1971, John Ehrlichman telephoned

General Cushman to ask the CIA to assist Howard Hunt in his undisclosed mission of burglarizing Dr. Fielding's office. In June 1972, when the White House was trying to use the CIA to head off the FBI investigation of Watergate, Nixon specifically directed that General Walters, rather than Helms, should be the contact man with Acting FBI Director Gray. When Walters subsequently balked at having the CIA pay salaries and put up bail money for the Watergate burglars, Dean testified that Ehrlichman directed him to press Walters further: "General Walters seems to have forgotten how he got where he is today."

Helms and the two generals had all "gone into the bag" for the Nixon White House. But the Watergate Committee, because it felt they were more sinned against than sinners, made no effort to highlight their small surrenders and evasive explanations.

In order to guard against the development of a secret police, the 1947 law establishing the CIA expressly forbade the agency from engaging in any espionage, intelligence-gathering, police work, or any other activity within the United States. Yet when Ehrlichman called General Cushman and asked him "to lend a hand" to Howard Hunt, he agreed. To protect himself, he taped the conversation. The tape showed they had time to chat about how each tried to stay in good physical condition by jogging and exercise, but Cushman was careful not to ask the vital question whether the mission on which Hunt needed help involved an American citizen and would take place in the United States. If either were true, it would be unlawful for the agency to assist Hunt. As a good bureaucrat, Cushman informed Helms of the Hunt interview. By refusing to intervene, Helms gave his assent. Only later, when Hunt made additional demands on the CIA, did Helms tell Cushman to call Ehrlichman and say they did not want to cooperate further.

When Senator Ervin asked Helms whether it "didn't strike you as strange" that the White House had hired Hunt for an undercover mission, Helms made this disingenuous reply: "Well, you know, Senator Ervin, at that time there was no intimation that this was even undercover work. What I understood Mr. Hunt had told General Cushman was that he wanted to conduct an interview and there was no intimation that this was undercover work."

But what Hunt asked for and received were false identification papers and physical disguises including a wig and a voice-altering mechanism. How undercover would a mission have to be before an old CIA hand like Helms got intimations?

In early January 1973, as the Justice Department was preparing for the trial of the Watergate burglars, it requested the CIA to summarize all its contacts with Hunt. The CIA telephoned General Cushman, who by then had left to become Marine Commandant, for his recollections. In an astonishing bit of weaseling, Cushman over the next month gave three different versions. He first told the CIA that he had seen Hunt at Ehrlichman's request. Then the CIA reported that Ehrlichman, having learned through Justice of what Cushman said, had protested its accuracy. Would Cushman prepare a memorandum on the specific point, the CIA asked.

In a memorandum of January 8, 1973, Cushman wrote: "I received a call over the White House line from either Mr. Ehrlichman, Mr. Colson, or perhaps Mr. Dean (I simply cannot recall at this late date just which one it was) stating that Mr. Hunt would call on me."

On January 10, after a telephone call from Ehrlichman, Cushman prepared another memorandum and omitted any names: "I cannot recall at this late date who placed the call, but it was someone with whom I was acquainted as opposed to a stranger."

Yet all the while, Cushman knew that a tape recording existed of his interview with Hunt in which both of them mentioned Ehrlichman's intervention. The Watergate Committee released that tape, and General Cushman recanted the January 10 memorandum. But the committee passed over in silence the question of whether the head of the Marine Corps might have suppressed evidence in a memorandum to the Justice Department.

At the request of the White House, Helms in 1971 permitted the CIA staff psychologists to prepare a psychological profile of Daniel Ellsberg. Such profiles are normally prepared only of foreign leaders. Since Ellsberg is an American citizen, the CIA had again broken the law. Helms told the Committee that he had "genuine regrets about being pressured" into assisting in the anti-Ellsberg project.

Against the background of these earlier small concessions, it seems a most likely proposition that Nixon thought he could hush up the Watergate affair by passing it off as a CIA operation. To this end, Ehrlichman and Haldeman called Helms and Walters to the White House on June 23, 1972. Although Helms and Walters knew and from the outset had stated to the White House that Hunt and the arrested Cubans had no connection with any CIA operation in Mexico, they played along with this fiction and delayed the FBI investigation of the "laundering" of Watergate funds through Mexico for two critical weeks. After the meeting, and at Haldeman's direction, General Walters went to Gray and told him that "the continuation of the FBI investigation in Mexico might uncover some covert activities of the Central Intelligence Agency." In doing so, Walters exceeded Helms's instructions and misled Gray. After the White House meeting, Helms had told Walters to say nothing to Gray except to remind him that there is an FBI–CIA agreement that if either runs into the operations of the other, it is to desist and notify the other agency. Walters, however, did more than convey to Gray the message that Haldeman had instructed him to deliver. According to Gray's testimony (which on this point disputes that of Walters), Walters allowed him to

160

think that the "hands off Mexico" warning came directly
from the CIA and did not mention the meeting with the
White House aides. It was not until Gray asked on July 5
that this request be put in writing that Walters backed
off and told Gray on July 6 that this supposed risk
had no basis in fact.

Of the senior figures in the Watergate debacle, L. Patrick
Gray III was easily the most pathetic. A retired Navy
captain with twenty years' service, Gray still wears his
Naval Academy class ring. While doing congressional
liaison work for the Pentagon, he met Nixon when the
latter was vice president. Practicing law while in
retirement, Gray kept in touch with Nixon. When Nixon
became president, Gray entered the Justice Department.
In the spring of 1972 he had just been nominated to
be deputy attorney general when J. Edgar Hoover died,
and the President made him Acting Director of the FBI.
He was in his new job only four weeks when Watergate
broke. Gray had no law-enforcement experience. He
told the Watergate Committee: "I have not been
suspicious of people. I have not lived nor was I raised or
brought up with or served with people that I had
to be suspicious of."

  By the time he appeared as a witness, Gray was
a broken man. He now knew that Nixon had said of him
that he was such a poor witness at his confirmation
hearing that he probably did not have the brains to run
the FBI. He now knew that Ehrlichman had expressed
the opinion during those same confirmation hearings
that the Administration "ought to let him hang there, let
him twist slowly, slowly in the wind." Gray had not only

161

General Robert E. Cushman, Jr.

lost the coveted FBI directorship but he also faced
possible indictment for destroying evidence in the
Watergate case. With mournful visage and earnest voice,
Gray told how Ehrlichman and Dean had called him to
the White House and handed him two of Howard Hunt's
files that were "political dynamite" and "should never
see the light of day."

"The clear implication of the substance and
tone of their remarks was that these two files were to
be destroyed," Gray said.

After keeping the files for six months, he
burned them with the Christmas trash.

Gray testified that after his conversation on
July 6, 1972, with General Walters, he decided to warn
Nixon that something fishy was going on. Interestingly, he
decided the surest way to reach him was to call Clark
MacGregor, the President's new campaign manager. It
worked. Nixon, who was in San Clemente, called
him back promptly.

I just blurted out to him, "Mr. President, there is something
that I have to speak to you about.

"Dick Walters and I feel that there are people on your staff who
are trying to mortally wound you by using the FBI and the CIA
to confuse the question of whether or not there is CIA interest
or noninterest in people that the FBI wishes to interview."

163

L. Patrick Gray III

There was a slight pause and then the President said to me, "Pat, you continue to conduct your thorough and aggressive investigation."

Nearly nine months later, Gray had another telephone conversation with Nixon. This was "the typical buck-up type of call" in which the President expressed sympathy for the hard time Gray had been having in his confirmation hearings and assured him there would always be a place for him in the Nixon Administration. Then Nixon said, "Pat, remember, I told you to conduct a thorough investigation."

"I had an eerie feeling. I thought—he is trying to put that on the record, so to speak. Why?"

Gray did not know then that Nixon's conversations in San Clemente were not taped and that those in the White House were.

"In the service of my country, I withstood hours and hours of depth charging, shelling, bombing, but I

165

never expected to run into a Watergate in the service of a President of the United States," Gray sadly told the Committee.

Friday the thirteenth of July may have been a critically unlucky day for Richard Nixon. On that day, Alexander P. Butterfield, while being routinely interrogated in private by a member of the Watergate Committee staff, was asked whether it was possible, as John Dean suspected, that his final conversation with Nixon had been secretly taped. After a considerable pause, Butterfield replied that it had been taped because all of the President's conversations in his offices in the White House and the Executive Office Building were automatically taped.

Butterfield, a career Air Force officer, had retired as colonel in 1969 when his old friend H. R. Haldeman invited him to join the White House staff as his deputy and secretary to the Cabinet. Butterfield had been rewarded for more than four years of White House service by his appointment in March 1973 as head of the Federal Aviation Administration. A Nixon loyalist, Butterfield was chagrined at discovering that his truthfulness had given the Committee critical information it had not previously possessed.

"I only hope that I have not by my openness and by my adherence to all instructions received to date, given away something which the President planned to use at a later time in support of his position," he told the committee.

Would Butterfield have kept silent about the taping if Haldeman had thought to give him such instructions? The question is unanswerable. But among

166

Alexander P. Butterfield

the papers in the Haldeman files subpoenaed by the Watergate Committee was one from Butterfield concerning Ernest Fitzgerald, an Air Force civilian employee striving to regain the job from which he had been fired because he had publicly blown the whistle about the Air Force's wasteful purchasing practices.

Butterfield's memorandum to Haldeman read in part: "Fitzgerald is no doubt a topnotch cost expert but he must be given very low marks in loyalty; and after all, loyalty is the name of the game. . . . We should let him bleed, for a while at least. Any rush to pick him up and put him back on the federal payroll would be tantamount to an admission of earlier wrongdoing on our part."

Of Richard G. Kleindienst it could be said that nothing became him like adversity. As a former attorney general forced by the Watergate scandals to resign after less than ten months in office, Kleindienst was a good-humored, reasonably candid witness for the Committee. In his previous five years in Washington as John Mitchell's deputy and during his brief tenure as attorney general, he had shown himself to be politically minded, ethically calloused and, as a witness in history's longest confirmation hearing, alternately arrogant or evasive.

When Robert Carson, the administrative assistant to Republican Senator Hiram Fong of Hawaii, approached him with an offer of a $100,000 campaign contribution if a certain individual were not prosecuted, Kleindienst either did not realize or did not care that he had been offered a bribe until several days later when he

discovered that a criminal case had been developed against Carson. Kleindienst then rushed to submit a memorandum to the FBI detailing the conversation.

Kleindienst had been badly burned by his involvement in the settlement of the ITT antitrust case. That controversy greatly prolonged his confirmation hearing through the winter and spring of 1972 as Kleindienst, Mitchell, and other Administration witnesses dodged and turned in an effort to explain their numerous contacts with ITT officials and lobbyists and to account for the Justice Department's irregular handling of the case.

Once he finally became the nation's chief law officer, Kleindienst publicly defended the FBI's slipshod investigation of the Watergate case but privately tried to keep himself uninvolved. His public comments could sometimes be astonishing. Interviewed in September 1972 on public television by Elizabeth Drew, he was asked about reports that CREEP officials had systematically destroyed files which tied the Nixon campaign organization to the Watergate burglary.

In reply, Kleindienst said: "I don't know whether they [the records] had been destroyed or not. . . . And then the destruction of documents by a campaign committee or a corporation doesn't necessarily mean that the law has been violated. . . . I'm not connected with the campaign committee. I don't know what they did. I don't know the circumstances. I don't know the facts."

Now Kleindienst sat amid the ruins of his career with nothing much to defend or explain away. Chain-smoking, occasionally throwing one leg over the arm of his chair, and toying with a matchcover stamped "Caesar's Palace, Las Vegas," he sold himself to the

169

Richard G. Kleindienst

Committee as a direct, commonsensical fellow who had rebuffed improper pressures from the White House staff throughout the Watergate case. He had refused to intervene to get the burglars released on the first day of their arrest, had refused John Dean's request to see the FBI interviews in the Watergate investigation (a request later incautiously granted by Pat Gray without Kleindienst's knowledge), and had rejected Ehrlichman's complaints about Justice Department subordinates. When he learned in April 1973 of the involvement of Mitchell and other close friends, he had the good sense to realize that he had no choice except to resign. The announcement of his resignation was delayed only because of Nixon's desire to have an additional name to bracket with those of Ehrlichman and Haldeman in his April 30 speech and thereby create the false impression that he—Nixon—was conducting a big housecleaning.

Kleindienst's most significant testimony concerned a luncheon with Dean and Ehrlichman in January 1973, near the end of the Watergate trial, in which Ehrlichman questioned him at length about sentencing procedures and the chances of getting the Watergate defendants placed on probation. Kleindienst subsequently checked with Assistant Attorney General Henry Petersen of the Criminal Division, who was supervising the Watergate prosecutors. In his own testimony, Petersen recounted his conversation with Kleindienst: "We rode out to the airport and he said, 'I just had lunch with Dean and Ehrlichman and they raised a question of whether or not leniency could be accorded these defendants.' And I said, 'Absolutely not.' . . .

"We discussed more what the procedure was, the sentencing procedure, and when they would be

sentenced and what have you, and he finally said, 'Do me a favor, go on back and go on over to the White House and tell those crazy guys over there what you just told me before they do something they will be sorry for.'"

Since the members of the Committee and the staff were physically exhausted as the first phase of the hearings drew to an end, they did an increasingly ragged job of cross-examination. In their questioning of Kleindienst and Petersen, they failed to follow up this highly suggestive testimony. What were those "crazy guys" at the White House planning to do that "they will be sorry for"? The luncheon took place when Hunt's demands were escalating and when Dean through Caulfield was desperately trying to keep McCord from breaking away from the conspiracy. If Ehrlichman and Dean had been able to obtain an assurance of leniency for the defendants, they could more easily sustain the cover-up. Failing to obtain that assurance, they had no "goody" to dangle before Hunt and McCord except a promise of presidential clemency. Since only the president can confer clemency, an offer of clemency is one of the critical issues in determining Nixon's involvement in the conspiracy to obstruct justice.

Petersen came on strong before the committee as God's angry man. He testified in a crisp colloquial style and seemed to have the tang of a natural human personality rather than the uneasiness and control of a role player. In a husky voice, Petersen expressed "resentment" at the appointment of Special Prosecutor Cox to replace him as head of the Watergate investigation because it was a reflection on the integrity and competence of himself and the rest of the Justice Department.

Henry E. Petersen

According to his own testimony, Petersen had been refreshingly blunt in his conversation with the President. "I said, 'If I reach the point where I think you are involved, I have got to resign. If I come up with evidence of you, I am just going to waltz it over to the House of Representatives.' But I said, 'What is important is that my wife, who is no left-wing kook, is raising these questions of me and that indicates to me that you have got a most serious problem.' "

Petersen was potentially a critically important witness. He had been John Dean's contact at the Justice Department. He knew the entire story of what went on inside the Department throughout the Watergate investigation. But in less than three hours of cursory examination, the Committee failed to probe for weak spots in Petersen's testimony or to reconcile contradictions between his testimony and that of other witnesses. To what extent, if any, did he suspect from the first that Dean was directing a cover-up to protect those above him at the White House? Why, according to Dean's testimony, did he describe Magruder's perjured testimony before the grand jury with the suggestive phrase, "he got through by the skin of his teeth"? Why did he write a letter to the House Banking Committee to try to head off its investigation of Watergate before the November 1972 election? What concerns prompted him when he said on April 26, 1973, according to Gray's recollection, " 'Pat, I am scared.' And I said, 'Henry, why?' And . . . he said, 'I am scared because it appears that you and I are expendable and Haldeman and Ehrlichman are not.' "

Petersen, a career government employe, told the Committee: "I've been there [the Justice Department] too long to jeopardize my reputation

173

for anybody."

   But honest men at the CIA had bent a little to accommodate the prevailing winds from the Nixon White House. Whether and to what extent Petersen had done so remains an unexplored question.

Howard Hunt was the Committee's first witness when it resumed hearings on September 24 and the last witness to testify concerning the Watergate burglary and the cover-up that followed. A thin, almost wispy man of medium height with long fingers and a long, Cyrano-like nose, Hunt wore a cheap, tan, wash-and-wear suit that accentuated the sallow complexion produced by six months' imprisonment. For twenty-one years he had dwelled in the amoral world of espionage as a CIA agent. For an even longer time, first as a movie script writer and later as a prolific weekend writer of paperback spy thrillers, he had dwelled in that same world in his imagination. His testimony made it immediately clear that disgrace and imprisonment had not altered his outlook.

   "I was an intelligence officer—a spy—for the Government of the United States," he proudly told the Committee.

   He was unrepentant and unconcerned as he recounted in a high, light voice his participation in the burglary of Dr. Fielding's office, the Watergate break-in, the abandoned plan to steal political documents from the safe of a Las Vegas publisher, the search for embarrassing information about Senator Edward Kennedy, and the doctoring of State Department cables to make it appear as if President Kennedy had ordered the murder of President Diem of South Vietnam.

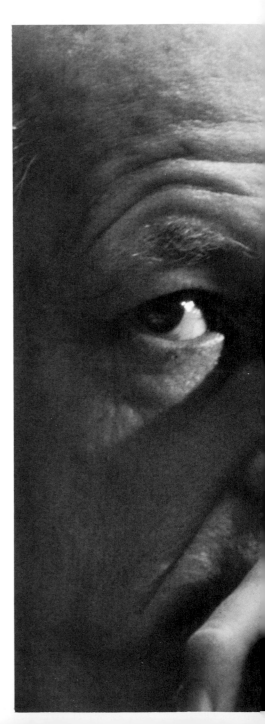

Hunt seemingly made no distinction between espionage against the nation's foreign enemies and espionage against domestic political opponents, or between the fantasies sketched out in his own fiction and the deeds of his daily life. As Linda Charlton of *The New York Times* wrote, "He was Walter Mitty rewritten to Graham Greene."

Having pleaded guilty and kept silent at his trial, while milking the White House for all he could get in cash payments and promises of future clemency, Hunt now coolly abandoned his former patrons. Prior to his public appearance, he had cooperated with state prosecutors in California in the preparation of their indictments against Ehrlichman, Krogh, and others for the Fielding burglary and had escaped indictment himself. Now, before the Committee, Hunt skewered Colson, who had recommended him for his White House job. He testified that he had shown Colson photographs taken inside Dr. Fielding's office, but Colson had refused to look at them, remarking, "I don't want to hear anything about it." Furthermore, he testified that Colson "was aware of the over-all intelligence plan" that culminated in the Watergate break-in and had conversed with G. Gordon Liddy about it.

Both these pieces of testimony could be damaging to Colson, who had repeatedly denied knowledge of both episodes. But they would be helpful to Hunt in getting his indeterminate sentence reduced because they showed he was now cooperating with authorities. In the enveloping mood of every man for himself, these small human betrayals were only to be expected. The Watergate affair was ending in the moral squalor in which it had begun.

175

Howard E. Hunt, Jr.

Mrs. Dean

Mrs. Magruder

Mrs. Sloan

WIVES

Four wives came to the Caucus Room to share the public ordeal of their husbands. Three took "the wife's seat" behind and to the right of their husbands. The fourth, Jo Haldeman, sat with her daughter in the front row of spectators.

Each wife seemed to mirror personal qualities of her husband. Gail Magruder, a mother of four small children, had the cool good looks of a post-debutante suburban matron married to an ambitious young marketing executive. What unkind trick of fate had brought her to political Washington, D.C., rather than secure Darien or Winnetka? Deborah Sloan had a bride's intensity and devotion and the thin, well-bred attractiveness of her husband, who tried to maintain a gentleman's honor in a very rough crowd. Stamped on the strong face of Jo Haldeman, married for twenty-four years and mother of nearly grown children, were the habits of reserve and deep personal discipline to be expected in the partner of Nixon's relentless chief of staff.

During her husband's five days of testimony, Maureen Dean became the most familiar of the wives. Her good looks, glistening blond hair, and jeweled fingers conveyed an air of glamour, but she equaled her husband in her total composure under stress.

And Martha Mitchell, the most famous wife, the only one to comment on the substance of Watergate, the one who provided manic glimpses of the dark truth, was the wife who never appeared.

Mrs. Haldeman and daughter

177

THE CRISIS

The Watergate crisis tested the American people, their political leadership, and their institutions.

The Senate Watergate Committee, a makeshift and unpredictable institution, met the test. None of its members was a brilliant interrogator or masterly in pulling together diffuse bits of evidence. Four of its seven members—Ervin (North Carolina), Baker (Tennessee), Talmadge (Georgia), and Gurney (Florida)—were elected from the South, the region where Richard Nixon was politically strongest and where votes were risked in opposing him. The Committee yielded somewhat in mid-course to Nixon-generated pressures to speed up its hearings, meeting five days a week instead of three, sitting longer each day, and confining its questions to ten-minute relays. As a result, the Committee and its staff became physically overtaxed, its questioning of some of the later, major witnesses ragged and unprepared.

Yet the Committee achieved its central purpose. It educated the Congress and the country about the threat that Nixon and his men had developed against the integrity of elections, against limited, constitutional government, against the liberties of the people. A corrupt and lawless style of government is now summed up in the word Watergate.

Mr. Justice Holmes once remarked that people may "need education in the obvious more than investigation of the obscure." The Ervin Committee did both. It turned up some startling information that had previously been obscure or completely unsuspected: a White House "enemies list" of individuals to be "screwed" by tax audits and government harassment; memoranda linking the President and other high officials with the suspicious settlement of the ITT antitrust case; the fact that tapes existed of virtually all White House telephone calls and conversations.

The Committee also educated everyone in the obvious: that a president is sworn to enforce the laws, not break them; that the Fourth Amendment means what it says when it declares that the "right of the people to be secure in their persons, houses, papers and effects, against

unreasonable searches and seizures, shall not be violated"; and that
the phrase "national security" is not a magic code dissolving the restraints
of the Constitution. With the powerful help of commercial and public
television, the Committee conducted an informal adult education course
in the Constitution. Its hearings made most of the participants in the
complicated Watergate drama into familiar persons in millions of
living rooms. If Americans had not watched those thirty-seven days of
Senate hearings from May to August, there would not have been the
explosion of constructive indignation in October over the ouster
of Special Prosecutor Archibald Cox.

The Nixon Administration orchestrated a campaign to
discredit the Committee. Spiro Agnew, before he was unmasked, derided
the hearings as a "rain dance" and a "Perry Masonish" performance.
Senator Carl Curtis of Nebraska said the Committee was wasting its
$500,000 budget and not "serving any lawful purpose." Secretary of the
Interior Rogers Morton deplored the Committee "because there's too
big a tendency to try people in a forum that is not designed for that."

This campaign to "shut down the hearings" never caught
hold, although there were times in August and September 1973 when it
seemed about to. The very amateurishness of the Senators in their
investigative efforts, their genial inconsequence (so frustrating to some
viewers), and their courtesy to all the witnesses reassured millions of
ordinary citizens that the hearings were, indeed, an honest attempt
to get at the truth and not a frivolous or fanatical political scalping party.
Friendly critics might sometimes complain that Counsel Sam Dash's
questioning was not pointed or persistent enough, but hostile critics
could not convince anyone that the mild, earnest Mr. Dash was
imitating a Grand Inquisitor.

"It's not the function of this Committee to get every pound
of flesh," Dash told an interviewer midway in the hearings. "My goal is
to present these hearings in a professional, calm manner. I don't want
the stigma of the McCarthy hearings where everyone invoked the
Fifth instead of answering."

180

The Watergate hearings achieved something much more
important than a pound of flesh or the humiliation of any witness.
It helped to change the mind of the nation.

Whenever the Senate hearings began on May 17,
1973, Watergate appeared to be in the same category as the Justice
Department scandals that had plagued Harry Truman in his last eighteen
months in office or the Sherman Adams affair in the Eisenhower
Administration—that is, a situation that damaged the President
politically and distressed him personally, but no more than that. When
the hearings ended on August 7, it was evident that Watergate was a
catastrophe that could bring down the President.

On May 22, Nixon issued a 4,000-word statement setting forth
his defense. It was obviously designed to anticipate and respond to the
devastating testimony that the White House by then knew John Dean
was presenting to the U.S. Attorney and the Watergate Committee.
In the statement, Nixon admitted that he had ordered the wiretapping
of approximately twenty newsmen and White House employees from
1969 to 1971. He conceded that he had approved the so-called Huston
Plan for secret "bag jobs" (breaking, entering, and burglarizing of
selected targets), illegal mail covers, illegal wiretaps, and other irregular
procedures against domestic radicals, but had rescinded his approval
after J. Edgar Hoover's protests. He acknowledged that in 1971 he had
established the White House Special Investigations Unit, the plumbers
who were to plug leaks "and to investigate other sensitive security
matters." He further conceded that he had tried to restrict the FBI
investigation of Watergate by instructing Haldeman and Erlichman
"to insure that the investigation of the break-in not expose either an
unrelated covert operation of the CIA or activities of the White House

Investigations Unit.''

It was an extraordinary document. For the first time in American history, a President admitted ordering illegal acts. It was a looking-two-ways document. He repeatedly acknowledged responsibility in some large, impersonal sense but disavowed blame in any direct, human sense. He frequently indicted himself and exonerated himself in the same paragraph. A typical passage concerned the chain of command he established for the plumbers:

I looked to John Ehrlichman for the supervision of this group. Egil Krogh, Mr. Ehrlichman's assistant, was put in charge. . . . The unit operated under extremely tight security rules. Its existence and function were known only to a very few persons at the White House. . . . I told Mr. Krogh that as a matter of first priority, the unit should find out all it could about Mr. Ellsberg's associates and his motives. Because of the extreme gravity of the situation . . . I did impress upon Mr. Krogh the vital importance to the national security of his assignment. I did not authorize and had no knowledge of any illegal means to be used to achieve this goal. However . . . I can understand how highly motivated individuals could have felt justified in engaging in specific activities that I would have disapproved had they been brought to my attention.

If the group's existence was known only to "a very few persons" and if the President personally briefed not only the group's supervisor (Ehrlichman) but its young operating chief (Krogh), why wasn't everything of importance brought to the President's attention? Who else but the President had given these "highly motivated individuals" the idea that they could run around committing burglaries and be protected?

The May 22 statement was a huge dud. There was none of the spirit of Fiorello LaGuardia's famous remark: "When I make a mistake, it's a beaut." Each grudging admission was coupled with a denial of specific knowledge or of specific personal responsibility or decorated with a useful legal loophole. It was not the statement of a national leader sure of his own mind and his own position. Nixon's downward slide had begun.

For nearly five months, through April, May, June, July, and the first half of August, Nixon kept his silence. He failed to attend church

The press

confident Nixon "putting Watergate behind him" and turning to the business of the people.

But casting a pall over all this was the headlong collapse of Spiro Agnew. Between August and October, Agnew fell from forthright, combative, conservative Mr. Clean to common tax evader. It was the week of October 15 before Nixon was able to finally push the dead whale of Agnew out of sight.

And down almost every corridor of power that Nixon ventured, there stared back the patient face of Nemesis in crewcut and bow tie: Special Prosecutor Cox.

In separate lawsuits, Cox and the Watergate Committee were suing Nixon for the right to listen to the tapes of his Watergate-related conversations in 1972–73, tapes whose existence had only become known from Alexander Butterfield's testimony on July 13. In response to Ervin's original request, Nixon wrote a letter of refusal in which he admitted the tapes were at least ambiguous. "As in any verbatim recording of informal conversations, they contain comments that persons with different perspectives and motivations would inevitably interpret in different ways," he wrote.

Commenting on this "rather remarkable letter," Ervin said, "You will notice the President says he has heard the tapes or some of them and they sustain his position. But he says he is not going to let anybody else hear them for fear they might draw a different conclusion. In other words, the President says they are susceptible of, as I construe it, two different interpretations, one favorable to his aides and one not favorable to his aides."

When the dispute reached the courts, Cox was in a stronger legal position than the Senate Committee because, as a member of the executive branch, he could not be attacked by Nixon's lawyers for violating the separation of powers among the three branches of government. Moreover, Cox was acting in behalf of a grand jury, a fact to which courts always attach special weight. Judge John Sirica delayed action on the Senate Committee suit and then ruled on procedural grounds that

he had no jurisdiction. But in Cox's suit, he ruled promptly that the President would have to turn the tapes over to the court for its inspection to determine whether there were any valid grounds for excluding all or portions of the tapes from the special prosecutor and the grand jury. The Court of Appeals affirmed Sirica's decision.

The concept of "executive privilege," if it applied to anything, surely applied to a president's personal conversations. But what if the conversations dealt with the commission of crimes? That novel question had never arisen in the courts. Nixon's lawyers declared: "The issue here is starkly simple: will the presidency be allowed to continue to function?"

If the grand jury were to hear the tapes of nine Nixon conversations, "the damage to the institution of the presidency will be severe and irreparable." If the courts were displeased by the President's refusal to hand over the tapes, they could do nothing. If the Congress were displeased, it would have to impeach him because "in the exercise of his discretion to claim executive privilege, the President is answerable to the nation but not to the courts."

The courts did not buy Nixon's I-am-only-trying-to-save-the-presidency argument. Neither did the public. Although the public opinion polls throughout the summer and early autumn continued to show a substantial majority of the American people against Nixon's impeachment and much divided and uncertain about the degree of his involvement in Watergate, they also showed overwhelming sentiment in favor of his "coming clean" and releasing the tapes. Through the noise and clamor of the constitutional argument, people could recognize a man trying to hide something.

In a series of intricate negotiations during the week beginning Monday, October 15, Nixon strove to find a way out. His predicament was not only how to protect the tapes but also how to rid himself of Cox. In addition to the Watergate burglary and cover-up, the special posecutor was investigating the suspicious circumstances of the ITT antitrust settlement, the activities of the "plumbers," and the large sums of cash raised by the White House throughout Nixon's first term in

188

office, including two donations of $50,000 in cash from businessman Howard Hughes to C. G. "Bebe" Rebozo, the President's intimate friend.

Nixon's solution to the predicament was an offer to provide summaries of the disputed tapes to the Senate Committee and to Judge Sirica. The accuracy of these tapes would be vouched for by Senator John Stennis of Mississippi, who would be the only person to hear the actual tapes. In exchange for these summaries, Cox was to agree not to go to court in the future to seek other tapes or any written notes, memoranda, or other materials in the President's files. It was an offer that Nixon knew Cox would have to refuse. Summaries of tapes might be sufficient for a grand jury to indict but would not meet the requirements of any judge in an actual trial. Moreover, no self-respecting prosecutor would voluntarily agree to restrict the kinds of evidence he might seek.

It would seem that Nixon's strategy was to force Cox to resign, but in such circumstances that the country would accept his departure. If Judge Sirica did not accept the summaries as sufficient, the nine tapes could later be yielded to him. With Cox gone, the multiple investigations being conducted by the special prosecutor could be brought back under the control of the Justice Department, where they might be more easily managed or, alternatively, a new, more docile special prosecutor could be appointed who would stop poking around in the White House files.

One cover for this maneuver would be Senator Stennis's good reputation. Stennis was enlisted. Another cover would be the endorsement of Senators Ervin and Baker on behalf of the Watergate Committee. They were approached and proved amenable. As they later defensively explained, they felt the Committee had nothing to lose by accepting the summaries since its lawsuit had poor prospects in the courts. Moreover, Ervin was under the impression that except for deletions of national security information, the summaries would actually be verbatim transcripts. Whether that was the firm understanding of all the other participants to the agreement never became clear.

What is remarkable is that Ervin and Baker acted without

consulting the other members of the Committee, that they acted upon a verbal understanding rather than insisting upon a written agreement signed by Nixon, and that they seem never to have inquired how this arrangement might affect the work of the special prosecutor.

Nixon's strategy may have appeared audacious to him and his small coterie of advisers as it evolved in the week of October 15–19, but it could work only if Cox in the critical moment proved indecisive and everyone else were complaisant.

In reality, nothing went right for Nixon. Cox conducted a masterful press conference that laid out the issues without personal rancor and in a way that every citizen could understand. The top level of the Justice Department turned out to contain not one but two men of integrity, as Attorney General Elliot Richardson and Deputy Attorney General William Ruckelshaus resigned in protest. And across the country public opinion roared up in a "firestorm" of outrage. In four days, members of the House and Senate received 350,000 telegrams, almost all of them calling for Nixon's impeachment. The nation's newspapers, having backed Nixon overwhelmingly for reelection less than a year earlier, were now sharply critical. The legal profession joined the struggle; the president of the American Bar Association and the deans of seventeen law schools denounced the firing of Cox and Nixon's attempt to provide Judge Sirica with summaries instead of the actual tapes that the court had ordered. Organized labor called for Nixon's impeachment. Nixon had attempted a self-protective coup on Friday, October 19, and Saturday, October 20; the country that weekend answered him with a roar of public disapproval.

When even the lax and timorous leadership of the House of Representatives decided to begin impeachment, Nixon retreated. On Tuesday, October 23, his lawyers told Judge Sirica that they would hand over the tapes. But it was too late. The firing of Cox and the public reaction on that fateful weekend had brought the long drama of Watergate to its crisis.

As usually happens in a political crisis, the truth becomes the simpler explanation, the one that all the people can readily grasp. Those who are avoiding the truth or trying to suppress it have the cleverer, more complicated argument, the one harder to explain and to comprehend. In an unformulated but unmistakable way, the people had reached a collective judgment that Nixon could no longer be trusted. They did not want him to preside from the White House over the nation's bicentennial in 1976 as Ulysses Grant had presided over its blighted centennial—a reproach to himself and to the nation that had tolerated him.

Only the denouement remained to be acted out. More hysterical press conferences: "I can take it . . . the tougher it gets, the cooler I get . . . outrageous, vicious, distorted reporting . . . I am not a crook." More surprises: two of the tapes were missing because they never existed. Another deception or truth's ironic revenge? It hardly mattered.

Had it all been a tragedy? Surely not in any classic sense. "Pity is occasioned by undeserved misfortune," Aristotle observed. The tragic hero has to be brought from happiness to misery "not by any depravity but by some great error on his part." With Nixon, however, the error was not on his part but on others'. If the voters had rejected the mean demagoguery of his first campaigns for the House and the Senate, if the Republican Party had heeded the editorial counsel of the *Washington Post* and the old *New York Herald-Tribune* and dropped him from the national ticket in 1952 after his first secret slush fund was exposed, if General Eisenhower had followed through on his own doubts and denied him renomination in 1956, if the healthy instinct of the electorate to reject him for president in 1960 and for Governor of California in 1962 had been respected by party leaders, if the national opposition within his own party had been more intelligent and energetic

in 1968 or if Lyndon Johnson had not laid waste his own party by the war in Vietnam, Nixon would never have entered the presidency. It took the weaknesses of many other men and several accidents of history to open the way to power. Many among his political peers in both parties had known from the first that he was unworthy of the nation's highest office. So Nixon's fall from public grace failed to provide the catharsis of tragedy; rather, there was only a sense of weary relief.

The human consequences of Watergate diminished rather than enlarged everyone, participants, press chorus, and spectators alike. The brutal words quoted by Bart Porter in his Senate testimony convey the quality of this impoverishing experience. Porter testified that when he learned that the Watergate cover-up was coming apart and that his own perjury would be exposed, he turned for help to James Sharp, one of the lawyers for the Committee to Reelect the President.

"I explained very quickly what I have just explained to you gentlemen here and he looked at me rather incredulously and he said, 'My God, you are an ant.' He said, 'You are nothing.' He said, 'Do you realize the whole course of history is going to be changed?' "

Although it was no tragedy in classical human terms, Watergate was a political tragedy for America. For 180 years, the office of the presidency had been kept inviolate. It had been well understood that no matter what crimes or follies a man had committed on his way to the White House, once he was ensconced there, he tried to rise above his past and keep faith with the people's trust. Grant might be coarse and uncomprehending, Arthur might have been a cynical dispenser of patronage, Harding and Truman might have risen through malodorous party machines, and Johnson might have enriched himself while in the Congress, but once each of them took the oath of office as President, he remembered whose house he lived in and what tradition he was trustee of and what responsibilities were now his.

What Richard Nixon and Spiro Agnew did was to bring the vulgar corruption of local and state government to the very summit of the national government for the first time. What had been encountered so often and fought against so often by reformers—the bribe-taking, the cynical deals, the brazen lies and cover-ups of the big-city bosses and the county courthouse "rings," of the suburban zoning commissioners and the state legislators with "For Sale" signs on their consciences—all this had now drifted up into the Oval Office and the Executive Office Building.

Nixon and Agnew worsened their positions by their self-exculpatory justifications. "Everybody does it!" they cried, defaming the whole craft of politics. Thus, President Nixon said on April 30, "I know that it can be very easy, under the intensive pressures of a campaign, for even well-intentioned people to fall into shady tactics, to rationalize this on the grounds that what is at stake is of such importance to the nation, and that the end justifies the means. And both of our great parties have been guilty of such tactics." But the cold intrigues that led to Watergate and the calculated deceits to conceal them cannot be ascribed to the warm excess of partisan conviction. In reality, Nixon had surrounded himself with very few professional politicians; most of his sad young men, his political agents and bagmen, his compromised bureaucrats, his image experts and propaganda spokesmen learned what little they knew of high politics in his service. Charles Evans Hughes, trying to restore the Republican Party's reputation after the Harding scandals, said, "Guilt is personal and knows no party." Guilt is still personal and knows no profession or calling.

It would be tragic if Watergate produced only a new anti-politics, a more pervasive distrust of public life and everyone in it. Feebler democracies have died from passivity and easy cynicism; those are the qualities that demagogues and would-be dictators exploit. Not everyone in America loves freedom. There are those who would enjoy being bosses in a police state, others who would be willing to do its dirty work, and still others who would acquiesce in tyranny for the sake of stability. Watergate failed because it was an inept and slovenly conspiracy, its authoritarian impulse feeble. But in other hands the outcome might have been different. As the novelist James T. Farrell has written:

196

"Watergate One failed. But what about Watergate Two? . . . It will be perilous for us to forget that in the years ahead, there can be a Watergate Two. And if there is, we should best assume that it will be more carefully planned, and that the lessons of the bungled Watergate One will have been well learned."

The power of the national government is not going to diminish very much, if at all, and politics are not going to go away. In the struggle to prevent corrupt government and to avoid the far worse menace of police-state government, Americans can find no safety in privacy and despair. In the future as in the past, honest government and individual liberty can survive only if there are intelligence, vigilance, and courage to sustain them.